W9-BZV-230

Praise for *The Myths of Innovation*

"The naked truth about innovation is ugly, funny, and eye-opening, but it sure isn't what most of us have come to believe. With this book, Berkun sets us free to try to change the world, unencumbered with misconceptions about how innovation happens."

> —Guy Kawasaki, author of The Art of the Start

"Brimming with insights and historical examples, Berkun's book not only debunks widely held myths about innovation, it also points the way toward making your new ideas stick. Even in today's ultra-busy commercial world, reading this book will be time well spent."

> —Tom Kelley, GM, IDEO; author of The Ten Faces of Innovation

"*The Myths of Innovation* is insightful, inspiring, evocative, and just plain fun to read. And on top of that it goes to the heart of innovation and its many challenges. It's totally great."

> —John Seely Brown, former Chief Scientist of Xerox, and Director, Xerox Palo Alto Research Center (PARC); current Chief of Confusion

"I love this book! On every page—actually, in every paragraph—the reader experiences a mind-changing moment. Scott Berkun is a master demythologizer, and even though one is left sitting among the debris of previously cherished beliefs, the overall effect is enriching, comforting, inspiring. Wise, witty, packed with fascinating history, compelling anecdotes, and priceless ideas, it equips the reader with a posture toward promoting innovation that will simply leave other managers behind, terminally encumbered by their reliance on discredited myths. A must read."

> —Richard Farson, President, Western Behavioral Sciences Institute; author of Management of the Absurd: Paradoxes in Leadership

"Berkun unravels the misconceptions of where ideas come from with wit, realism, and authority. This book will change the way you think about invention—permanently."

> —Gina Trapani, Lifehacker.com

"Would-be trailblazers and worldchangers should stop waiting for lightning to strike their laptops and study the wisdom Scott Berkun has gathered instead. Methodically and entertainingly dismantling the clichés that surround the process of innovation, Berkun reminds us that there are no shortcuts to breakthroughs, and that creativity is its own reward."

—*Scott Rosenberg, author of* Dreaming in Code, *and cofounder of Salon.com*

"If you care about being innovative, whether for yourself, your company, or your students, you need to know where the truth lies— what the myths are. Scott Berkun's book dispels the myths while providing solid advice about the practice. All this in an eminently readable, enjoyable style that delights as it informs. Small, simple, powerful: an innovative book about innovation."

—*Don Norman, Nielsen Norman Group, Northwestern University; author of* Emotional Design *and* Design of Everyday Things

"No word in the current business arena is more used with incorrect applicability than the word *innovation*. Scott's tome is understandable, thoughtful, often contrarian, and a great read."

—*Richard Saul Wurman, author of* Information Anxiety, *and creator of the TED conferences*

"This book cuts through the hype, analyzes what is essential, and more importantly, what is not. You will leave with a thorough understanding of what really drives innovation."

—*Werner Vogels, CTO, Amazon.com*

"This book shatters the sacred cows of innovation myths and gives real-world innovators insight into making innovations that matter."

—*Jim Fruchterman, CEO, Benetech; 2006 MacArthur Fellow*

"Berkun shows us what innovation isn't, challenging our preconceived notions of what innovation means. Whether you agree or disagree with Scott, this book will make you think."

—*Gary William Flake, Ph.D., Founding Director, Microsoft Live Labs*

"Berkun looks into innovation myths and reveals how they can damage true organizational creativity. He reveals the myths but also provides an incredibly useful framework for going forward—this is an awesome book."

—*Tara Hunt, Founder, Citizen Agency*

"This book is a wake-up call for both business people and technologists alike. It dispels many of the misguided notions about how innovation works and lets us all come to a better understanding of just what innovation means and how it can create change in the world."

—*David Conrad, Studio Director, Design Commission, Inc.*

"How I ran a startup without reading this book baffles the mind."

—*Richard Stoakley, CEO, Overcast Media, Inc.*

"As individuals, corporations, and nations struggle to master the increasing technological and social complexities of the modern world, a deeper understanding of the mechanisms of innovation is required to make effective policy and business decisions. Berkun's approachable and fast-paced book provides an excellent introduction to the issues involved while demolishing common misconceptions and leaving the reader hungry to learn more."

—*Cory Ondrejka, CTO, Linden Lab, creators of* Second Life

"Essential reading for designers, technologists, thinkers, and doers: if you want to learn how and when to really innovate, read this book."

—*James Refill, Design Manager, Search & Social Media Group, Yahoo!*

"A quick and engaging read. Exposes the realities faced by successful inventors, debunks silver-bullet solutions others wish were true, and offers real approaches for making things that transform our lives."

—*Bo Begole, Manager, Ubiquitous Computing Lab, PARC Research*

"*The Myths of Innovation* is not just funny, perceptive, and useful—it's downright inspiring!"

—*Erin McKean, Editor, Oxford American Dictionary*

"I loved this book. It's an easy-to-read playbook for people wanting to lead and manage positive change in their businesses."

—*Frank McDermott, Marketing Manager, EMI Music*

"Berkun's guide to innovation is straightforward, succinct, and highly engaging. Use once and be glad. Use regularly and dramatically increase your odds of success."

—*Douglas K. Smith, author of* Make Success Measurable! *and* Fumbling the Future: How Xerox Invented, Then Ignored, the First Personal Computer

"Berkun's latest book is a readable analysis of the history of innovation and popular misconceptions. His myth debunking will help innovators, managers of innovative teams, or funders of innovative activities. I'm buying copies for my entire lab."

—*Michael N. Nitabach, Assistant Professor, Department of Cellular Physiology, Yale University School of Medicine*

the myths of innovation

the myths of innovation

scott berkun

O'REILLY®

Beijing • Cambridge • Farnham • Köln • Paris • Sebastopol • Taipei • Tokyo

The Myths of Innovation
by Scott Berkun

Copyright © 2007 Scott Berkun. All rights reserved.
Printed in Canada.

Published by O'Reilly Media, Inc., 1005 Gravenstein Highway North, Sebastopol, CA 95472.

O'Reilly books may be purchased for educational, business, or sales promotional use. Online editions are also available for most titles (*safari.oreilly.com*). For more information, contact our corporate/institutional sales department: (800) 998-9938 or *corporate@oreilly.com*.

Editor: Mary Treseler O'Brien
Production Editor:
    Marlowe Shaeffer
Copyeditor: Marlowe Shaeffer

Proofreader: Reba Libby
Indexer: Ellen Troutman Zaig
Interior Designer: Ron Bilodeau
Illustrator: Robert Romano

Printing History:

May 2007:   First Edition.

ISBN-10: 0-596-52705-5
ISBN-13: 978-0-596-52705-1
[F]

Contents

Preface

*By idolizing those whom we honor
we do a disservice both to them and
to ourselves…we fail to recognize
that we could go and do likewise.*

—Charles V. Willie

Prefaces are often like bad first dates: too much talk, too soon. Books, like future significant others, should know how much to say and when. Chapter 1 gets the first slot for a reason: if I've done my job, you can start with its first sentence and continue until you hit the back cover. That said, I offer you the choice of skipping the rest of the preface and digging in, or skimming around. It's the only way to know if we're right for each other. I hope we are, but if you don't like what you find, it's me, not you.

The aims of this book

The goal is to use myths about innovation to understand how innovations happen. Each chapter discusses one myth, explores why it's popular, and then uses the history of innovations—recent and ancient—to explain the truth. Although debunking and demystifying does take place, the intent is to clarify how innovation happens so that you'll better understand the world around you and can avoid mistakes should you attempt innovation yourself. My job as author is to:

1. Identify myths about innovation.

2. Explain why they're popular.

3. Explore and teach from the truth.

The book takes on business, scientific, and technological innovation all at once, striking at the roots of the innovation tree more than the branches. Even if you are aware of many of the myths, you won't be bored by their dissection; the related truths are often more interesting than the myths themselves.

Assumptions I've made about you

This book is written for anyone interested in how we got where we are, why things are how they are, and what people in the present can do to be innovators themselves. It's a crossover book covering business, history, culture, and technology. There are no prerequisites of knowledge, and I use examples from science, history, the arts, politics, and just about everything else to show how these myths and truths are relevant to all.

1. You are curious and want to learn.

2. You don't want to be hit over the head with jargon and statistics.

3. You are open to being challenged and considering alternative points of view.

4. You have a sense of humor and learn more if you smile now and then.

The research accuracy commitment

I've done my best to support claims with evidence and separate opinion from fact. However, as you'll learn in Chapter 2, history is not what we think it is. Despite my best efforts, the nature of history makes it possible that I have misrepresented facts or distorted the work of others. I promise that any oversights were unintentional, and I believe that my arguments and the thoughts they provoke are valuable despite any inaccuracies. I'll do my best after the book's publication to update future editions with any corrections or improved references as I'm made aware of them; I will also note them at *http://www.mythsofinnovation.com*. If you want details on the research process used, see the back of this book.

How to use this book

In Chapter 6, it's revealed that there are, in fact, many uses for this book, but the simplest one is that you start at the top, read, and then work your way down, repeating on the following pages. Seriously, if a book requires an instruction manual, something very bad has happened.

The only note is that the chapters are highly independent and can be read individually. However, the ordering is intentional and some points benefit from their predecessors.

And now, since you were patient enough to read this entire preface, I'll get out of the way. Enjoy and stay in touch.

—Scott Berkun
Redmond, WA
www.scottberkun.com

CHAPTER 1

The myth of epiphany

While waiting in the lobby of Google's main building, I snuck into the back of a tour group heading inside. These outsiders, a mix of executives and business managers, had the giddy looks of kids in a candy factory—their twinkling eyes lost in Google's efforts to make a creative workplace. My clandestine activities unnoticed, we strolled together under the high ceilings and bright-colored open spaces designed to encourage inventiveness. No room or walkway was free of beanbag chairs, Ping-Pong tables, laptops, and Nerf toys, and we saw an endless clutter of shared games, brain-teasing puzzles, and customized tech gadgetry. The vibe was a happy blend of MIT's Media lab, the Fortune 500, and an eccentrically architected private library, with young, smart, smiley people lingering just about everywhere. To those innocents on the tour, perhaps scarred survivors of cubicle careers, the sights at Google were mystical—a working wonderland. And their new-found Google buzz was the perfect cover for me to tag along, observing their responses to this particular approach to the world of ideas (see Figure 1-1).

Figure 1-1. One of the creative interiors of Google's main campus in Mountain View, California.

The tour offered fun facts about life at Google, like the free organic lunches in the cafeteria and power outlets for laptops in curious places (stairwells, for example), expenses taken to ensure Googlers are free, at all times, to find their best ideas. While I wondered whether Beethoven or Hemingway, great minds noted for thriving on conflict, could survive such a nurturing environment without going postal, my attention was drawn to questions from the tourists. A young professional woman, barely containing her embarrassment, asked, "Where is the search engine? Are we going to see it?" to which only half the group laughed. (There is no singular "engine"—only endless dull bays of server computers running the search-engine software.)

The second question, though spoken in private, struck home. A thirty-something man turned to his tour buddy, leaning in close to whisper. I strained at the limits of trying to hear without looking like I was eavesdropping. He pointed to the young programmers in the distance, and then, behind a cupped hand, he wondered, "I see them talking and typing, but when do they come up with their ideas?" His buddy stood tall and looked around, as if to discover something he'd missed: a secret passageway, epiphany machines, or perhaps a circle of black-robed geniuses casting idea spells. Finding nothing, he shrugged. They sighed, the tour moved on, and I escaped to consider my observations.

The question of where ideas come from is on the mind of anyone visiting a research lab, an artist's workshop, or an inventor's studio. It's the secret we hope to see—the magic that happens when new things are born. Even in environments geared for creativity like Google, staffed with the best and brightest, the elusive nature of ideas leaves us restless. We want creativity to be like opening a soda can or taking a bite of a sandwich: mechanical things that are easy to observe. Yet, simultaneously, we hold ideas to be special and imagine that their creation demands something beyond what we see every day. The result is that tours of amazing places, even with full access to creators themselves, never convince us that we've seen the real thing. We still believe in our hearts there are top-secret rooms behind motion-sensor security systems or bank-vault doors with ideas, tended by their shaman-like keepers, stacked up like bars of wizardly gold.

For centuries before Google, MIT, and IDEO, modern hotbeds of innovation, we struggled to explain any kind of creation, from the universe itself to the multitudes of ideas around us. While we can make atomic bombs and dry-clean silk ties, we still don't have satisfying answers for simple questions like: Where do songs come from? Is there an infinite variety of possible kinds of cheese? How did Shakespeare and Stephen King invent so much, while we're satisfied watching sitcom reruns? Our popular answers have been unconvincing, enabling misleading, fantasy-laden myths to grow strong.

One grand myth is the story of Isaac Newton and the discovery of gravity. As it's often told, Newton was sitting under a tree, an apple fell on his head, and the idea of gravity was born. It's entertaining more than truthful, turning the mystery of ideas into something innocent, obvious, and comfortable. Instead of hard work, personal risk, and sacrifice, the myth suggests that great ideas come to people who are lucky enough to be in the right place at the right time. The catalyst of the story isn't even a person: it's the sad, nameless, suicidal apple.

It's disputed whether Newton ever observed an apple fall. He certainly was never struck by one, unless there's secret evidence of fraternity food fights while he was studying in Cambridge. Even if the apple incident took place, the telling of the story discounts Newton's 20 years of work to explain gravity, the feat that earned him the attention of the world. Newton did not discover gravity, just as Columbus didn't discover America: the Egyptian pyramids and Roman coliseums prove that people knew the workings of gravity well before Newton. Instead, he explained, through math, how gravity works; while this contribution is certainly important, it's not the same as discovery.

The best possible truth to take from the apple myth is that Newton was a deeply curious man who spent time observing things in the world. He watched the stars in the sky and studied how light moved through air, all as part of his scientific work to understand the world. It was no accident that he studied gravity. Even if the myth were true and he did see an apple fall, he made so many other observations from ordinary things that his thinking couldn't have been solely inspired by fruity accidents in the park. Yet, that's the lesson we're encouraged to take.

Newton's apple myth is a story of epiphany or "a sudden manifestation of the essence or meaning of something,"[1] and in the mythology of innovation, epiphanies serve an important purpose. The word has religious origins, and its first use meant that all insight came by divine power, as in "My epiphany from God can save the village!" This isn't surprising, as most early theologians,[2] including Christians, defined God as the sole creative force in the universe. As a rule, people believed that if it's creative, it's divine, but if it's derivative, it's human. Had you asked the first maker of the wheel[3] for an autograph, he'd be offended that you'd want his name on his work, instead of his god's (one wonders what he'd think of Mr. Goodyear and his eponymous tires).[4]

Today, we use epiphany without awareness of its heavy-duty heritage, as in, "I had an epiphany for organizing my sock drawer!" While the religious connotations are forgotten, the implications remain: we're hinting that we don't know where the idea came from and aren't willing to take credit for it. Even the language, that an idea comes to us, or that we have to find ideas, puts them outside us, like ghosts or spirits, beyond our control. This way of thinking is helpful when we want to dissuade our guilt for blank sheets of paper where love letters, business plans, and novels are supposed to be, but it does little to improve whatever creative talents we have.

The Greeks were so committed to ideas as supernatural forces that they created an entire group of goddesses, not one but nine, to represent creative power. These nine goddesses, or *muses*, were the recipients of prayers from writers, engineers, and musicians. Even the great minds of the time, like Socrates and Plato, built shrines and visited temples dedicated to their particular muse (or for those who hedged their bets, muses). Right now, under our

---

1   This approximates the third entry in *Merriam-Webster's* online listing. The first two are religious in nature: *http://www.m-w.com/dictionary/epiphany*.

2   Robert S. Albert and Mark A. Runco, "A History of Research on Creativity," in *Handbook of Creativity*, ed. Robert J. Sternberg (Cambridge University Press, 1998), 16–20.

3   The wheel's prehistoric origins are a misnomer. The first wheels used for any practical purpose are believed to be about 5,000 years old. Start with *http://www. ideafinder.com/history/inventions/wheel.htm*.

4   The rubber tire was once a big innovation, and the history of Goodyear is a surprisingly good read: *http://www.goodyear.com/corporate/history/history_ overview.html*.

very secular noses, we honor these beliefs in our language, as words like museum (place for the muse) and amusement (inspiration by the muse) bear the Greek heritage of ideas as superhuman forces.

When amazing innovations arise and change the world today, the first stories about them mirror the myths from the past. Putting accuracy aside in favor of echoing the epiphany myth, reporters and readers first move to tales of magic moments. Tim Berners-Lee, the man who invented the World Wide Web, explained:

> *Journalists have always asked me what the crucial idea was or what the singular event was that allowed the Web to exist one day when it hadn't before. They are frustrated when I tell them there was no Eureka moment. It was not like the legendary apple falling on Newton's head to demonstrate the concept of gravity...it was a process of accretion (growth by gradual addition).*[5]

No matter how many times he relayed the dedicated hours of debate over the Web's design, and the various proposals and iterations of its development, it's the myth of magic that journalists and readers desperately want to recreate.

When the founders of the eBay Corporation[6] began, they struggled for attention and publicity from the media. Their true story, that the founders desired to create a perfect market economy where individuals could freely trade with each other, was too academic to interest reporters. It was only when they invented a quasi-love story—about how the founder created the company so his fiancée could trade PEZ dispensers—that they got the press coverage they wanted. The truer story of market economies wasn't as palatable as a tale of muse-like inspiration between lovers. The PEZ story was one of the most popular company inception stories told during the late 1990s, and it continues to be told despite confessions from the founders. Myths are often more satisfying to us than the truth, which explains their longevity and resistance to facts: we want to believe that they're true. This begs the question: is shaping the truth into the form of an epiphany myth a kind of lie, or is it just smart PR?

---

[5] Tim Berners-Lee, *Weaving the Web* (HarperCollins, 1999).
[6] Adam Cohen, *The Perfect Store: Inside eBay* (Little, Brown and Company, 2003).

Even the tale of Newton's apple owes its mythic status to the journalists of the day. Voltaire and other popular 18th-century writers spread the story in their essays and letters. An eager public, happy to hear the ancient notion of ideas as magic, endorsed and embellished the story (e.g., the apple's trajectory moved over time, from being observed in the distance to landing at his feet to eventually striking Newton's head in a telling by Disraeli[7] decades later). While it is true that by dramatizing Newton's work, Voltaire helped popularize Newton's ideas, two centuries later, little of Newton's process is remembered: myths always serve promotion more than education. Anyone wishing to innovate must seek better sources and can easily start by examining the history of any idea.

Ideas never stand alone

The computer keyboard I'm typing on now involves dozens of ideas and inventions. It's comprised of the typewriter, electricity, plastics, written language, operating systems, circuits, USB connectors, and binary data. If you eliminated any of these things from the history of the universe, the keyboard in front of me (as well as the book in front of you) would disappear. The keyboard, like all innovations, is a combination of things that existed before. The combination might be novel, or used in an original way, but the materials and ideas all existed in some form somewhere before the first keyboard was made. Similar games can be played with cell phones (telephones, computers, and radio waves), fluorescent lights (electric power, advanced glass moldings, and some basic chemistry), and GPS navigation (space flight, high-speed networks, atomic clocks). Any seemingly grand idea can be divided into an infinite series of smaller, previously known ideas.

Similar patterns exist in the work of innovation itself. For most, there is no singular magic moment; instead, there are many smaller insights accumulated over time. The Internet required nearly 40 years of innovations in electronics, networking, and packet-switching software before it even approximated the system

---

[7] Isaac Disraeli, *Curiosities of Literature: With a View of the Life and Writings of the Author* (Widdleton, 1872).

Tim Berners-Lee used to create the World Wide Web.[8] The refrigerator, the laser, and the dishwasher were disasters as products for decades before enough of the barriers—cultural and technological—were eliminated, each through insights of various kinds, to make them into true business innovations. Big thoughts are fun to romanticize, but it's many small insights coming together that bring big ideas into the world.

However, it's often not until people try their own hands at innovation or entrepreneurship that they see past the romance and recognize the challenges for what they are. It's easy to read shallow, mythologized accounts of what Leonardo da Vinci, Thomas Edison, or Jeff Bezos did, and make the mistake of mimicking their behavior in an entirely different set of circumstances (or with comparatively modest intellects). The myths are so strong that it's a surprise to many to learn that having one big idea isn't enough to succeed. Instead of wanting to innovate, a process demanding hard work and many ideas, most want to have innovated. The myth of epiphany tempts us to believe that the magic moment is the grand catalyst; however, all evidence points to its more supportive role.

The best way to think about epiphany is to imagine working on a jigsaw puzzle. When you put the last piece into place, is there anything special about that last piece or what you were wearing when you put it in? The only reason that last piece is significant is because of the other pieces you'd already put into place. If you jumbled up the pieces a second time, any one of them could turn out to be the last, magical piece. Epiphany works the same way: it's not the apple or the magic moment that matters much, it's the work before and after (see Figure 1-2).

The magic feeling at the moment of insight, when the last piece falls into place, comes for two reasons. The first reason is that it's the reward for many hours (or years) of investment coming together. In comparison to the simple action of fitting the puzzle piece into place, we feel the larger collective payoff of hundreds of pieces worth of work. The second reason is that innovative work isn't as predictable as jigsaw puzzles, so there's no way to know

---

Figure 1-2. Epiphany is the moment when the last piece of work fits into place. However, the last piece isn't any more magical than the others, and has no magic without its connection to the other pieces.

when the moment of insight will come: it's a surprise. Like hiking up a strange mountain through cold, heavy fog, you never know how much further you have to go to reach the top. When suddenly the air clears and you're at the summit, it's overwhelming. You hoped it was coming, but you couldn't be certain when or if it would happen, and the emotional payoff is hard to match (explaining both why people climb mountains as well as why they invent new things).

Gordon Gould, the primary inventor of the Laser, had this to say about his own epiphany:

> *In the middle of one Saturday night...the whole thing...suddenly popped into my head and I saw how to build the laser...but that flash of insight required the 20 years of work I had done in physics and optics to put all of the bricks of that invention in there.*

Any major innovation or insight can be seen in this way. It's simply the final piece of a complex puzzle falling into place. But unlike a puzzle, the universe of ideas can be combined in an infinite number of ways, so part of the challenge of innovation is coming up with the problem to solve, not just its solution. The pieces used to innovate one day can be reused and reapplied to innovate again, only to solve a different problem.

The other great legend of innovation and epiphany is the tale of Archimedes' Eureka. As the story goes, the great inventor Archimedes was asked by his king to detect whether a gift was made of false gold. One day, Archimedes took a bath, and on observing the displacement of water as he stepped in, he recognized a new way to look at the problem: by knowing an object's volume and weight, he could compute its density. He ran naked into the streets yelling "Eureka!"—*I have found it*—and perhaps scandalizing confused onlookers into curious thoughts about what exactly he had been looking for.

The part of the story that's overlooked, like Newton's apple tale, is that Archimedes spent significant time trying and failing to find solutions to the problem before he took the bath. The history is sketchy at best, but I suspect he took the bath as stress relief from the various pressures of innovation.[9] Unlike Google employees, or the staff at MIT, he didn't have friends with Nerf weapons or sand volleyball courts to blow off steam. So, as is common in myths of epiphany, we are told where he was when the last piece fell into place, but nothing about how the other pieces got there.

---

[9] The most well-known version of the Eureka story comes in the form of a legend in Vitruvius' *Ten Books of Architecture* (Dover, 1960), 253–255. Of note is that this book is the first pattern language of design in Western history, documenting the Roman architecture techniques of Vitruvius' time.

In Mihaly Csikszentmihalyi's book, *Creativity: Flow and the Psychology of Discovery and Invention*,[10] he studied the thought processes of nearly 100 creative people, from artists to scientists, including notables like Robertson Davies, Stephen Jay Gould, Don Norman, Linus Pauling, Jonas Salk, Ravi Shankar, and Edward O. Wilson. Instead of doing clinical research with probes and brain scans, he focused instead on the innovators' individual insights. He wanted to understand their perceptions of innovation, unfiltered by the often stifling and occasionally self-defeating rigors of hard science.

One goal was to understand epiphany and how it happens; through his research, he observed a common pattern. Epiphany had three parts, roughly described as early, insight, and after.[11] During the early period, hours or days are spent understanding the problem and immersing oneself in the domain. An innovator might ask questions like: "What else in the world is like this?" and "Who has solved a problem similar to mine?" learning everything he can and exploring the world of related ideas. And then there is a period of incubation in which the knowledge is digested, leading to experiments and rough attempts at solutions. Sometimes there are long pauses during incubation when progress stalls and confidence wanes, an experience the Greeks would have called "losing the muse."

The big insights, if they happen, occur during the depths of incubation: it's possible these pauses are minds catching up with everything they've observed. Csikszentmihalyi explains that deep quiet periods, time spent doing unrelated things, often helps new ideas surface. Csikszentmihalyi wrote, "Cognitive accounts of what happens during incubation assume...that some kind of information processing keeps going on even when we are not aware of it, even while we are asleep." Our subconscious minds play large roles in creative thinking: they may be the sources for the unexplained insights we romanticize. When a promising idea surfaces out of the subconscious and rises into our active minds, it can feel like it came from somewhere else because we weren't aware of our subconscious thoughts while we were mowing the lawn.

---

[10] Mihaly Csikszentmihalyi, *Creativity: Flow and the Psychology of Discovery and Invention* (HarperPerennial, 1997).

[11] Csikszentmihalyi describes epiphany in five phases, but I've simplified it to three for the purposes of this chapter.

The best lesson from the myths of Newton and Archimedes is to work passionately but to take breaks. Sitting under trees and relaxing in baths lets the mind wander and frees the subconscious to do work on our behalf. Freeman Dyson, a world-class physicist and author, agrees, "I think it's very important to be idle...people who keep themselves busy all the time are generally not creative. So I am not ashamed of being idle." This isn't to justify surfing instead of studying: it's only when activities are done as breaks that the change of activity pays off. Some workaholic innovators tweak this by working on multiple projects at the same time, effectively using work on one project as a break from the other. Edison, Darwin, da Vinci, Michelangelo, and van Gogh all regularly switched between different projects, occasionally in different fields, possibly accelerating an exchange of ideas and seeding their minds for new insights.

One of the truths of both Newton's apple tale and Archimedes' bathtub is that triggers for breakthroughs can come from ordinary places. There is research that creative people more easily make connections between unrelated ideas. Richard Fennyman curiously observed students spinning plates in the Cornell University cafeteria and eventually related the mathematics of this behavior to an unsolved problem in quantum physics, earning him the Nobel Prize. Picasso found a trashed bicycle and rearranged its seat and handlebars, converting it into a masterpiece sculpture of a bull. The idea of observation as the key to insight, rather than IQ scores or intellectual prowess, is best captured by something da Vinci, whose famous technological inventions were inspired by observing nature, wrote hundreds of years ago:

> *Stand still and watch the patterns, which by pure chance have been generated: Stains on the wall, or the ashes in a fireplace, or the clouds in the sky, or the gravel on the beach or other things. If you look at them carefully you might discover miraculous inventions.*

In psychology books, the talent for taking two unrelated concepts and finding connections between them is called associative ability. In his book *Creativity in Science: Change, Logic, Genius, and Zeitgeist*, Dean Simonton points out that "persons with low associative barriers may think to connect ideas or concepts that have very little basis in past experience or that cannot easily be traced logically."[12] Read that last sentence again: it's indistinguishable from various definitions of insanity. The tightrope between being strange and being creative is too narrow to walk without occasionally landing on both sides, explaining why so many great minds are lampooned as eccentrics. Their willingness to try seemingly illogical ideas or to make connections others struggle to see invariably leads to judgment (and perhaps putting some truth to stereotypes of mad scientists and unpredictable artists). Developing new ideas requires questions and approaches that most people won't understand initially, which leaves many true innovators at risk of becoming lonely, misunderstood characters.

Beyond epiphany

If we had a list of the most amazing breakthrough insights that would change the world in the next decade, hard work would follow them all. No grand innovation in history has escaped the long hours required to take an insight and work it into a form useful to the world. It's one thing to imagine world peace or the Internet, something Vannevar Bush did in 1945 in a paper titled "As We May Think,"[13] but it's another to break down the idea into parts that can be built, or even attempted.

Csikszentmihalyi describes this part of innovation, the elaboration of an idea into function, as "...the one that takes up the most time and involves the hardest work." Scientists need to not only make discoveries, but to provide enough research to prove to others that the discoveries are valid. Newton was far from the first to consider gravity, but he was the only person able to complete the years of work. *Star Trek*, a television program in the '60s, had the idea for cell phones, but it took decades for technology to be developed and refined to the point where such a thing could be practical (and, of course, many of *Star Trek*'s sci-fi ideas have yet to be realized). Not to mention the services and businesses that are

---

[12] Dean Keith Simonton, *Creativity in Science: Chance, Logic, Genius, and Zeitgeist* (Cambridge University Press, 2004).

[13] Bush's paper is a recommended read. It goes beyond visionary hyperbole and breaks down a vision into smaller, practical problems (a hint for today's visionaries): *http://www.theatlantic.com/doc/194507/bush*.

needed to make the devices available affordably to consumers around the world. The big ideas are a small part of the process of true innovation.

The most useful way to think of epiphany is as an occasional bonus of working on tough problems. Most innovations come without epiphanies, and when powerful moments do happen, little knowledge is granted for how to find the next one. Even in the myths, Newton had one apple and Archimedes had one Eureka. To focus on the magic moments is to miss the point. The goal isn't the magic moment: it's the end result of a useful innovation. Ted Hoff, the inventor of the first microprocessor (Intel's 4004), explained, "...If you're always waiting for that wonderful break-through, it's probably never going to happen. Instead, what you have to do is keep working on things. If you find something that looks good, follow through with it."[14] Nearly every major innova-tion of the 20th century took place without claims of epiphany. The World Wide Web, the web browser, the computer mouse, and the search engine—four pivotal developments in the history of business and technology—all involved long sequences of innova-tion, experimentation, and discovery. They demanded contribu-tions from dozens of different individuals and organizations, and took years (if not decades) to reach fruition. The makers of Mosaic and Netscape, the first popular web browsers, didn't invent them from nothing. There had been various forms of hyper-text browsers for decades, and they applied some of those ideas to the new context of the Internet. The founders of Google did not invent the search engine—they were years late for that honor. As the founders at Amazon.com, the most well-known survivor of the late-90s Internet boom, explain, "There wasn't this sense of 'My God. We've invented this incredible thing that nobody else has seen before, and it'll just take over.'"[15] Instead they, like most innovators, recognized a set of opportunities—scientific, techno-logical, or entrepreneurial—and set about capitalizing on them.

---

[14] Kenneth A. Brown, *Inventors at Work: Interviews with 16 Notable American Inventors* (Microsoft Press, 1988).

[15] Paul Barton-Davis, quoted in Robert Spector, *Amazon.com: Get Big Fast* (HarperBusiness, 2000), 48.

Peter Drucker, in *Innovation and Entrepreneurship*,[16] offers advice for anyone in any pursuit awaiting the muse:

> *Successful entrepreneurs do not wait until "the Muse kisses them" and gives them a "bright idea": they go to work. Altogether they do not look for the "biggie," the innovation that will "revolutionize the industry," create a "billion-dollar business" or "make one rich over-night." Those entrepreneurs who start out with the idea that they'll make it big—and in a hurry—can be guaranteed failure. They are almost bound to do the wrong things. An innovation that looks very big may turn out to be nothing but technical virtuosity, and innovation with modest intellectual pretensions; a McDonald's, for instance, may turn into gigantic, highly profitable businesses.*

The same can be said for any successful scientist, technologist, or innovator. It's the ability to see a problem clearly, combined with the talent to solve it, that matters. Both of those tasks are generally defined, however unglamorously, as work. Epiphany, for all its graces, is largely irrelevant because it can't be controlled. Even if there existed an epiphany genie, granting big ideas to worthy innovators, they would still have piles of rather ordinary work to do to actualize those ideas. It is an achievement to find a great idea, but it is a greater one to successfully use it to improve the world.

---

16 Peter Drucker, *Innovation and Entrepreneurship* (Collins, 1993).

CHAPTER 2

We understand the history of innovation

History is written by those who win and
those who dominate.
—Edward Said

History is the lie commonly agreed upon.
—Voltaire

History is a damn dim candle
over a damn dark abyss.
—W. S. Holt

History is indeed the witness
of the times, the light of truth.
—Cicero

In the Egyptian wing of London's British Museum, I hovered by the Rosetta Stone, waiting for the guards to look away. When a child stumbled over the corner of a lesser relic, distracting the guards, I moved in. Holding my breath, I reached over the steel barrier, stretched out my trembling hand, and ran it across the letters on the Stone. My fingertips gently stroked the cold surface, racing along ancient corners of mysterious symbols: in one motion, I touched more history than fills many men's dreams. With my hand back at my side, I strolled away, ashamed and thrilled, praying against alarms and handcuffs that never came. I didn't wash that hand all day, lost in imagining the important men behind the Stone (see Figure 2-1).

But when the thrill of my museum mischief faded, one frustration remained: the Stone is famous for reasons irrelevant to those who conceived it. The stonecutters could not have imagined their work in a European museum 2,000 years in the future, with hired guards protecting it from hooligans like me. Yet, there it sat, as if its destiny was to be found in a rubble pile by the French, used to decipher hieroglyphics, and, finally, displayed in its true resting place in London. In the solemn, shrine-like atmosphere of the museum, I'd forgotten that the stone is an artifact: it's an object that was part of history but not history itself.[1]

---

[1] Today, the Stone is encased in glass. It was cleaned in 1998, removing layers of wax, inks, and oils collected over years of imprints, copies, and immature (cough) human patrons. The Stone is made of a substance similar to granite, immune to the negative effects of curious paws. On principle, I've since resisted the urge to make unauthorized contact with all relics, including history professors.

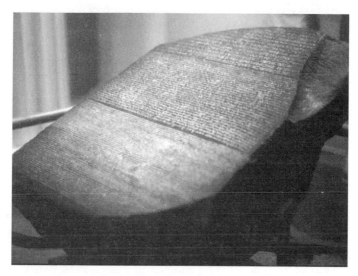

Figure 2-1. The Rosetta Stone at the British Museum, circa 1996.

Although the Stone is a more of a discovery than an invention, this gap between how the stonemakers saw their work and how we see it today is meaningful to innovators. To understand innovations as they happen, we need to see how history changes perceptions and re-examine events like the discovery of the Rosetta Stone.

Weighing nearly 2,000 pounds, the Stone is a fragment of an Egyptian pillar created in 196 BCE. In its time, the Stone was ordinary, one of many used by pharaohs to communicate with their people. The message on the Stone—the rarely mentioned reason it was made—is a public service announcement, mostly praising the pharaoh ("the new king, great in glory, the stabilizer of Egypt, pious in matters of gods, superior to his adversaries..."). The Stone is of minor interest save two facts:

1. When it was found in 1789, we were clueless about hieroglyphics.

2. It was the first object found with writing in both hieroglyphics and Greek, making translation possible.

It's a wondrous thing given our situation, but these facts have nothing to do with the making of the Stone—they're circumstances that developed lifetimes after its creation.

If we had sorted out hieroglyphics through other means, say, discovering an Egyptian-to-Greek translation book in Athens (possible, as the Greeks ruled Egypt for decades),[2] or finding another object written in multiple languages, it would have served the same purpose, replacing the Stone in the museum with something else (e.g., "The Rosetta recipe for Egyptian meatloaf"). So while the Stone deserves a first-rate exhibit in the British Museum, its value derives from great circumstances. The best lesson it offers is that ordinary things, people, and events are transformed into legends by the forces of time, all the time. Who knows: if I bury my beat-up third-rate cell phone into the right ditch in Paris, a million years from now, it might be the grand museum exhibit on some alien planet, as the cornerstone to (mis)understanding the human race ("Here, behind space-glass, is the historic Parisian phone").

What does all this have to do with innovation? Well, take one great innovation: the printing press. More than 500 years after his death, Johannes Gutenberg is heralded as one of the most important people in history. He's ranked above Einstein, Aristotle, and Moses in one list of the most influential people of all time.[3] Despite the fact that the Chinese invented movable type and many print techniques centuries earlier, Gutenberg was the first to succeed with them in Europe.[4] Today we can trace the existence of web sites and bestsellers directly to the work in his shop in Mainz, Germany.

However, the deception by omission in Gutenberg's story is that his influence was not felt in his lifetime. He was not a hero of his age, and, like the Rosetta Stone, his intentions were not the same as what we credit him for today. He was not trying to free the world through access to knowledge or pave the way for the Internet age: as best as we can tell, he was simply trying and

---

2   The famed library of Alexandria, the largest library of ancient times, may have had various tomes on translating hieroglyphics, but it was destroyed (probably in the 4th century): *http://www.bbc.co.uk/history/ancient/egyptians/*.

3   *http://www.answers.com/topic/the-100* based on the 1992 book by Michael H. Hart. *Time*'s 2006 Top 100 people lists a few innovation notables, including Jimmy Wales (Wikipedia) and Niklas Zennström and Janus Friis (the founders of Skype).

4   John Man, *Gutenberg: How One Man Remade the World with Words* (Wiley, 2002).

failing to make a living.[5] Like the stonecutters, Gutenberg was a craftsman doing his job, and he couldn't have imagined that centuries after his death, millions of books and web sites would be published annually, nor that they'd often mention his name.

His influence, similar to the impact of the Rosetta Stone, owes as much to circumstance, world politics, and chance as to his abilities as a printmaker. (The Chinese and Islamic civilizations both had the technological ingredients needed to achieve what Gutenberg did well before he was born, but it never came to be.[6]) Unlike Michelangelo, da Vinci, or other notables of his time, few records of Gutenberg's life were kept, as his work and life weren't deemed important: it's by a string of fortunate events that we even know his name.[7]

His innovations, in his time, were perceived in a radically different way than we see them now, which is a secret all innovators in the present must learn: when the legends we know so well today, from Vincent van Gogh to Steve Jobs to Albert Einstein, were becoming legendary, they were rarely seen as legends.

However, the stories told in schools and books present Gutenberg and other innovators as obvious, logical, and necessary contributors to the world, begging the assumption that if we were alive in their time, we'd see them the same way our history books portray. Or, that time would have stopped if they hadn't accomplished what we know them for. Those glorified accounts present innovation in a distorted way that is impossible to achieve because the neat arcs of progress, clear sense of purpose, and certainty of success are heavily shaped, if not invented, by hindsight.

---

5 Ibid. Most of what we do know of his life are court and business records, which show many failed projects and one major lawsuit in which Gutenberg lost much of his work.

6 The forces that made the difference were cultural and coincidental. The Chinese language had hundreds of characters, not 26, making printing systems harder to perfect. Gutenberg's work coincided with Luther's reformation of the Church, fueling interest in printing bibles—an interest that didn't surface in the East.

7 Ibid.

Why does history seem perfect?

If you take a walk in 21st-century Rome, it's obvious that Romans were masterful builders. There are coliseums (see Figure 2-2), temples, baths, and aqueducts thousands of years old, still standing (and in many cases still working). The problem is that we're biased by what we can't see. These buildings are the minority of what the Romans made: the others fell down or were built over, buried, or in some cases torn apart for materials used in other buildings and are thus lost to history. While the Romans deserve praise for their engineering prowess, they were not perfect engineers—they made mistakes all the time. Their ruling class did live in the glorious marble structures often shown in movies, but most Romans lived in collapse-prone tenements that killed thousands.[8]

Figure 2-2. The ever-sturdy Roman Coliseum, built over the remains of Emperor Nero's Golden House after the fire.

Despite the wonderful domes and legendary straight roads, the great fire of Rome in 64 CE burned down two-thirds of the city, including the 800-year-old Temple of Jupiter and the Atrium Vestae, the most sacred shrine in the Roman Forum.[9] This means

---

8 Jerome Carcopino, *Daily Life in Ancient Rome: The People and the City at the Height of the Empire* (Yale University Press, 2003).

9 *http://www.pbs.org/wnet/secrets/case_rome/index.html.*

that most of Rome we know today, ruins included, was built to replace the one that burned to the ground.

The lesson I'm hinting at is larger than Rome: examine any legend of innovation, from inventors to scientists to engineers, and you'll find similar natural omissions by history. History can't give attention to what's been lost, hidden, or deliberately buried; it is mostly a telling of success, not the partial failures that enabled success.[10] Without at least imagining the missing dimensions to the stories, our view of how to make things happen in the present is seriously compromised.

Recent history has similar problems. Most Americans are taught that Columbus was a hero who navigated dangerous seas to discover the place we call home, who fought for the supposedly innovative belief that the world was round. (This is a bizarre myth because sailors since ancient times knew the world was a sphere— the question was how large.[11]) But reading Howard Zinn's *A People's History of the United States*[12] or James W. Loewen's *Lies My Teacher Told Me*[13] reveals other equally relevant, but less flattering truths about Columbus, citing his involvement in genocide, grand incompetence, and rampant greed. Which view, hero or fool, is right? It seems they both are, but telling the truth requires more than the superficial paragraph historic figures like Columbus typically earn in textbooks. Perhaps worse, much like the myth of epiphany, we're fond of reading and writing histories that make us feel better about the present. Once learned, faith in those versions of history is hard to shake, no matter how strong the alternatives.

Consider this: would you buy a book titled *Why the Past Is Frustrating, Embarrassing, and Uncertain: A Litany of 78 Labyrinthine Enigmas*? It's hard to imagine this title on a bestseller list or

---

[10] In the case of Rome, few wrote about life in the tenements or chronicled engineering failures that occurred at the hands of the Roman elite (would you have published much about Caesar's or Nero's shortcomings?). Dissenting voices are rare in recorded history because few had the means to write (Rome is 1,500 years before Gutenberg's press). If history seems perfect, it's not because life made more sense to people then—it's because much is hidden about what happened and why.

[11] Aristotle was one of the first to suggest the idea, but any idiot in a boat observing the curve of the earth gets the idea. The horizon is approximately five miles away, further if you're elevated off the ground: *http://www-istp.gsfc.nasa.gov/stargaze/Scolumb.htm*.

[12] Howard Zinn, *A People's History of the United States* (HarperCollins, 1980).

[13] James W. Loewen, *Lies My Teacher Told Me* (Touchstone, 1996).

surviving a PTA review committee of material for elementary school students ("It will damage their little brains!", I can hear them crying). For all our interest in truth, we look to historians to sort things out, not to confuse or anger us. Holding up the Romans as superhuman, mistake-free engineers, or Columbus as the hero, simplifies the world in the same way as the myth of epiphany: it makes innovation special and separate from our daily experience. The Rosetta Stone, Gutenberg's press, and Roman architecture—all innovations or breakthroughs in their own way—arrived through many failures, chance events, and contrivances of human nature, but those details kill the easy romance we crave.

Don't get me wrong: we should feel wonder when near the Rosetta Stone, Roman ruins, or any stepping stone of innovation, but not because they're magical, otherworldly things (except, perhaps, the Egyptian pyramids, which we're still stumped by and couldn't replicate today).[14] Instead, we should be inspired because they connect our personal struggles, glories, fears, and passions with those of the people who made the things we're so quick to put on a pedestal—that's the true power of history.

Even with this goal, there are problems with the process of history that all historians, for all their integrity and altruistic intentions, can't escape: they have biases and desires like the rest of us. Beyond the need to make a living and write things people will buy, every writer, no matter how many degrees or textbooks in his name, has an opinion and a point of view (including yours truly). They can't study every fact or empathize with every perspective. These problems are so serious to innovation and general history that historians have a discipline to study them called *historiography*. Edward Carr, a prominent historian in this field, wrote in the classic *What Is History*:

> *It used to be said that facts speak for themselves. This is of course untrue. The facts speak only when the historian calls on them: it is he who decides to which facts to give the floor and in what order or context...a fact is like a sack—it won't stand up till you've put something in it.*[15]

---

[14] Johnathan Shaw, "Who Built the Pyramids," *Harvard*, http://www.harvardmagazine.com/on-line/070391.html.

[15] Edward Hallett Carr, *What Is History?* (Vintage, 1967).

The shocking secret, which explains why teachers torture children with endless trivia, is that there is no objective history. But teaching material that is palatable to everyone demands eliminating perspective, opinion, and humanity, leaving limp, soulless, humorless, embarrassment-free facts. Good histories are written by historians who carefully use diverse sources and take positions, but all histories are still based on interpretations and points of view. The good news is that even with accepted facts for events, there will always be new history books every year. The further we move away from an event, the more perspective we have about what happened. Just because we know all the facts about how the Internet was invented, or what started WWII, doesn't mean the history of those things ends. The more facts we compare and connections we make, the richer and more powerful history becomes.

The result is that our interests, as students of innovation, diverge with those of many historians and the general population. We want to understand the challenges of the past as if we were there, trying to innovate in that time with those constraints. We seek tactics to reuse or mistakes to learn from: we don't want convenience—we want truth. And to that end, there's no greater dispelworthy myth in the history of innovation than the idea that progress happens in a straight line.

Evolution and innovation

The Rosetta Stone sat buried in the sand, forgotten and unloved, for nearly 2,000 years. There were no markers or maps that led Napoleon's army to find it on that day in July.[16] There was plenty of time for someone else to destroy, deface, chop it into pretty sculptures, or hide it where it could never be found.[17] Of course, we're fortunate that events turned out as they did, but back then, when the past was the present, there was every possibility for it to turn out differently. The discovery of the Rosetta Stone was not inevitable.

---

[16] E. A. Wallis Budge, *The Rosetta Stone* (Dover, 1989), *http://www.napoleon-series.org/research/miscellaneous/c_rosetta.html*.

[17] One story related to Napoleon and Egypt is that his army was responsible for the destruction of the Sphinx's nose. This tale is definitely a myth: there are drawings of the damaged nose that date decades before Napoleon's Egypt visit.

Yet, when we look at any history timeline, we're encouraged to believe, by their omission, that other outcomes were impossible. Because the events on timelines happened, regardless of how bizarre or unlikely, we treat them today as preordained. It's not our fault, and it's not the fault of timeline makers (as that's a tough job). The simple fact is that these simplifications make history easier to explain. That said, it's also deceptive: at every point in every timeline in every book that will ever be published, there was as much uncertainty and possibility for change as there is today.

Consider how technology is taught in ages: first there was stone, then bronze, then iron; or, in the computer world, it's the ages of mainframes, personal computers, and the Internet. We label periods of time around discoveries/inventions, projecting onto the past an orderly map to what was, normal, average, everyday confusion. The earlier adopters of bronze swords, chasing the wooden-spear-wielding masses away from their treasures, didn't see themselves as being in the "Bronze Age" any more than the first Macintosh users saw themselves as being in the "pre-Internet Age" or than we see ourselves as being in the "age before telepathy was cheap and fun" (or whatever amazing thing happens next). Like in the present, people in the past believed they had divorced themselves from history and were living on the edge of the future in a crazy place called *now*.

This leads to the divisive question, the terrifying test of awareness of innovation history: were the innovations of the past inevitable? Are the Internet, the automobile, and the cell phone the necessary and unavoidable conclusion of human invention up until this time? Many think so. The idea even has the fancy name *techno-evolutionism*, but as cool as that sounds, it's still wishful thinking.[18]

Innovation and evolution demystified

This misconception of technological evolution mirrors a fallacy about the evolution of life, the universe, and everything. The unspoken myth many place inside the theory of evolution is that it defines modern civilization as the best possible result of history,

[18] *http://www.aber.ac.uk/media/Documents/tecdet/tdet10.html.*

since we're still around. Many think of evolution as a pyramid or ladder, with humans at the top, the crowning achievement of the planet, or even the universe (see Figure 2-3). But evolutionary science doesn't support this; like the pre-Copernican solar system, putting us at the center or on top of everything sure sounds nice, but it's absurd.

wrong   **right**

Figure 2-3. Evolution means only that what's on top is fit for the current environment, not that it's "better."

Natural selection doesn't mean that what's on top is special, it means only that the current environment is favorable toward that thing. Watch the music charts: Johnny Cash's album *Live at San Quentin* was a bestseller when released in 1968. For decades it didn't make the top 50, but, in 2005, when a successful movie was released about Cash's life, the environment changed.[19] The album—the same exact recording made nearly 40 years earlier— flew back up the charts: the criteria for the fittest changed. Certainly evolution is more complex than pop music (I hope so), but the shifting nature of what is dominant is similar.

While humans might be dominant today (though the ever-resilient insect population most species depend on questions this[20]), if the planet's temperature dropped by half, its nations blew everyone

19 *http://www.imdb.com/title/tt0358273/.*
20 Edward O. Wilson, *The Diversity of Life* (Belknap Press, 1992).

up, or a few medium-size asteroids crashed into the Atlantic, the fittest creatures won't be us. We'd be gone, best known by the surviving descendents of cockroaches as cute stuffed animals, in the same fashion we've eulogized our food chain-dominant predecessors, the dinosaurs.

I wish I had better news, but instead of a cozy timeline granting easy confidence in inevitable progress, there are no guarantees. The wonders of Greece and Rome didn't prevent our clumsy civilization-wide slide into the Dark Ages. Technologies are invented, lost, found, ignored, and then found again all the time. (For example, the secrets of concrete used in the Coliseum, shown in Figure 2-2, were lost when Rome fell, not to be rediscovered until the 1800s.[21]) Carr goes on to say, "no sane person ever believed in a kind of progress which advanced in an unbroken straight line without reverses and deviations and breaks in continuity." The dilemma is that, at any moment, it's difficult to know whether we're witnessing progress or merely, in a hill-climbing distraction, a short-term gain with negative long-term consequences. There have been many biological dead ends: more than 90% of all species in the history of the earth have become extinct, and that's after living for millions of years.[22]

Innovation follows: the reason we use mobile phones or personal computers isn't because they're necessarily better in the long run than smoke signals or cave paintings, or that they're at the top of an unshakable technology pyramid.[23] We've adopted these things gradually and intuitively as part of the experiment that is life. Simply because one thing has replaced another doesn't mean that it improves on it in every respect, and as conditions change, the notion of *improved* does as well. This hypothesis is easy to test: study the history of any innovation—from catapults to telegraphs to laser beams and nanotechnology—and you'll find its invention and adoption is based on ordinary, selfish, and mostly short-term motivations. Mistakes and complexities are everywhere, rendering a straight line of progress as a kind of invention itself.

---

[21] Dick Teresi, *Lost Discoveries* (Simon & Schuster, 2002).

[22] *http://pubs.wri.org/pubs_content_text.cfm?ContentID=519.*

[23] A simple review of misconceptions about evolution: *http://evolution.berkeley.edu/ evosite/misconceps/IBladder.shtml.*

Consider the gas-powered automobile, one of the most dominant technologies ever. In *The Evolution of Technology*, George Basalla explains:

> *There were no automotive experts at the turn of the century, only inventors and entrepreneurs following their hunches and enthusiasms and trying to convince potential car owners to buy their product. Given this situation, once the gasoline engine gained ascendancy, steamers and electrics were either forgotten or viewed as missteps along the road to automotive progress.*[24]

Gasoline engines and automobiles were successful not because they'd lead us on the best path, or even because they were the best solutions for the problems of the day. They succeeded, in natural-selection fashion, due to the combined circumstances of that time. Traffic jams, pollution, road rage, and dependence on limited oil supplies all call into question the suitability of the innovation we still base our lives on.

Dominant designs dominate history

Pick your favorite hot technology of the moment. How many different competing products are there? When an innovation is in progress, there are always competitors. Entrepreneurs are drawn to new markets because they have at least as good a chance as anyone else, even if they have less funding or experience. But what we forget is that every innovation, from a jet aircraft to a paper clip, was once an open, competitive, experiment-rich playing field.

In *Mastering the Dynamics of Innovation*, James Utterback writes:

> *It would be tempting to think that there is some predetermination to the emergence of dominant design—that automobiles with internal combustion engines were somehow exactly what the gods of transportation always meant for us to have, and that earlier experiments with electric and steam powered cars were misguided aberrations destined to go nowhere. The emergence of a dominant design is not necessarily predetermined, but is the result of the interplay between technical and market choices at any particular time.*[25]

[24] George Basalla, *The Evolution of Technology* (Cambridge University Press, 2002).

[25] James Utterback, *Mastering the Dynamics of Innovation* (Harvard Business School Press, 1996).

And don't forget the negative influence of the six-pack of human shortcomings: greed, irrationality, short-sightedness, egotism, lack of imagination, and just plain stupidity. It's quaint to think cars have seatbelts or antilock brakes because of the monk-like rationality, forethought, and good spiritedness of our innovation predecessors, but it just isn't so.[26]

This means that every technology, from pacemakers to contact lenses, fluorescent lights to birth control pills, arrived through the same chaos seen in the hot technologies of today. Just because dominant designs developed before we were born, or in fields so far from our own that we're ignorant of their struggles, doesn't mean their arrival was predictable, orderly, or even in our best interest. Yet, the dominant designs, the victors of any innovative pursuit, are the ones that get most of history's positive attention (see Figure 2-4).

Figure 2-4. A typical technology timeline (inspired by PBS).

In Figure 2-4, you can find a single blip in the 1980s representing when the personal computer (PC) came into existence. It's entirely polite and well behaved sitting there. You'll notice it doesn't take up more space than its neighbors, and it seems happy with its lot in life, perhaps sharing afternoon tea with its interesting friends the artificial heart and genetic engineering. But if we zoomed in, increasing the resolution so that the history of the PC was more

---

26 Ralph Nader's 1965 book, *Unsafe at Any Speed* (Grossman), revealed how collusion in the automotive industry prevented innovations in safety. See *http://www. answers.com/topic/unsafe-at-any-speed.*

than a single spot on a timeline, we'd see a chaotic, competitive, and unpredictable tangle of events. That happy little dot is a shill in the unavoidable deception that are timelines. Not only do timelines express a false omnipotent view of history, they're superficial, offering an illusion of comprehensiveness. History is deep, and, like a fractal, you can find much to see at different layers. Let's dig in and see where that little dot for the PC goes.

When the development of the PC began in the late 70s, there were many possibilities for how (and even if) it would be delivered to the world. Mainframes were the dominant design, and only a curious minority believed computers would be in people's offices, much less their homes. Apple Inc.'s 1977 release of the Apple II computer is credited with proving that there was a viable market for personal computers. However, Xerox PARC (a research institute at the copier company) developed an earlier personal computer, the Alto, in 1973. The door for the Apple II's success was opened when two things happened. First, two leading companies, Atari and Hewlett-Packard, rejected Apple's proposal to manufacture its computer for them.[27] Second, Xerox chose not to market the Alto, despite having plans in hand. Both facts seem stupid today, but that's hindsight talking; in most cases, Atari, Xerox, and HP made reasonable business decisions given the time.

If you made a rough sketch of the possibilities of personal computing in 1980, you'd have something like Figure 2-5. Unlike the timeline in Figure 2-4, the graph shows how many different possible simultaneous directions were pursued, each one challenging, inspiring, and feeding off the other. But the timeline hides all this action—the juicy chaotic details innovators need to understand.

And since the timeline must show a single date for the PC, the year 1983 was chosen: not 1973 (Alto), 1977 (Apple II), or 1979 (Atari 400). In 1982, the PC was popular enough for *Time* to name it Man of the Year (suggesting, perhaps, that I could run for gadget of the decade, though I suspect I won't be asked), but it was later on, around 1983, that the IBM PC was the true dominant design. The dot on the timeline is an amazing averaging of knowledge: it can't even hint at when the idea of the personal computer was first explored, or at the struggles the unnamed

---

[27] *http://www.islandnet.com/~kpolsson/comphist/.*

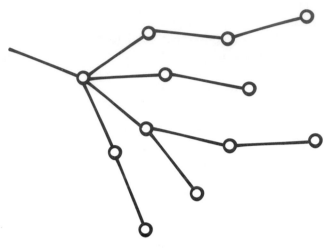

Figure 2-5. The tree of competing innovations.

pioneers of innovation had to overcome with electricity, mathematics, and transistors to pave the way for Apple, Atari, and IBM
to finish things off decades later.[28]

While the IBM PC did become the dominant design, we have to be
careful about drawing conclusions about why. It was never preordained, nor did it come solely because of IBM's monopolistic
dominance (they would release the comically stillborn PCjr soon
after).[29] It's worth considering what would have happened if
Xerox had chosen to release its Alto, or if Apple had convinced
Hewlett-Packard to bankroll their machine: IBM would not have
had the same opportunity. In the other direction, had Xerox or
IBM taken risks earlier, the PC timeline might have shifted forward, but without lessons learned from watching competitors, it's
possible that their immature products, launched before the technology or the culture was ready, could have set back the timeline
until 1985 or 2005 (see Figure 2-6).

Many innovations, such as the development of the web browser
almost 20 years after the PC, follow similar patterns of innovation. The first popular web browser was NCSA's Mosaic, released
in 1993 for the Windows operating system (the dominant-design

---

[28] A better, though still simple, timeline of the events that led to the personal
computer can be found at *http://inventors.about.com/library/blcoindex.htm*.

[29] *http://www.old-computers.com/museum/computer.asp?c=186*.

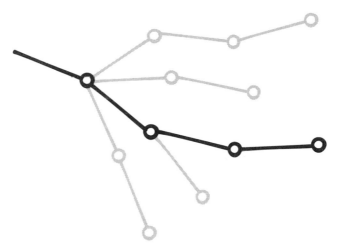

Figure 2-6. At best, timelines show only one path of the full tree of innovation history.

OS for the dominant-design IBM PC). Within two years, there were over a dozen competitors in the browser market; by 1997, the count was over 40.[30] In those early years, browsers were so prolific that other software, like word processors or games, often included a web browser made by that company. By 1997, two dominant players remained, Netscape Navigator and Microsoft Internet Explorer (disclosure: I worked on this product from 1994–1999), and they competed in what was grandly named the browser wars, with Internet Explorer becoming the dominant design by 1999. Few alternatives were popular until 2005 when the release of Mozilla Firefox—a reinvention of Netscape Navigator—started a new wave of interest and innovation in browser competition.

At this level of detail, there are many interesting questions. Why didn't the browser wars last longer? Did those years of intense competition work in the best interest of consumers, or are there more opportunities now, with an aging dominant design in place, for browsers like Firefox and the respectably resilient Opera

---

[30] A concise history of web browsers can be found at *http://www.livinginternet.com/w/wi_browse.htm*. For a deeper history of the hypertext systems web browsers were born from, see Jakob Nielsen, *Multimedia and Hypertext: The Internet and Beyond* (Morgan Kaufmann, 1995).

product to take larger risks and push another wave of innovation forward? And on it goes. The history behind personal computers and web browsers alone involves many books' worth of stories, decisions, inspirations, and surprises impossible to represent here, much less in one happy timeline-bound dot.[31] My point is that there are hundreds of similar dots on any timeline, at any scale, each with its own fascinating stories and lessons. You can zoom in on the story of, say, Apple, and again on any product or person involved, and find an entirely new set of insights and inspirations. (Try *www.folklore.org* for a fantastic start.)

But enough about history: it's one thing to explore why innovations of the past grew to dominance, but it's something else to innovate in the uncertainty of the present, which we'll explore next.

---

[31] For Xerox PARC, see Michael Hiltzik, *Dealers of Lightning: Xerox PARC and the Dawn of the Computer Age* (Collins, 2000); for Macintosh, see Steven Levy, *Insanely Great: The Life and Times of Macintosh, the Computer That Changed Everything* (Penguin, 2000); and generally, Paul Freiberger and Michael Swaine, *Fire in the Valley: A History of the Personal Computer* (McGraw-Hill, 1999).

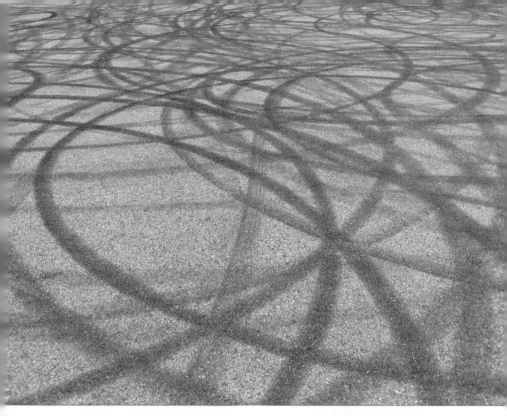

CHAPTER 3

There is a method for innovation

*By definition innovation is a charge
into the unknown.*
—Unknown

Every Tuesday morning, Mr. K., my chemistry teacher, stumbled into the high school science lab, unlocked the chemistry cabinet, and built the most destructive science experiments known to man. He would repeat these pyrotechnic feats, ignoring scorched desks and terrified students, until he passed out or ran out of ammunition. After demanding that we replicate his chemical prowess, he'd storm out of the room, rarely seen until the following week. I haven't lost my fear of Bunsen burners and glass vials, but I remember one concept important to all innovative pursuits that those experiments etched into my mind: methodology (see Figure 3-1).

Figure 3-1. A science teacher demonstrating the concept of methodology.

A method, as defined by the *American Heritage Dictionary*, is a systematic way of accomplishing something. I deduced from Mr. K.'s behavior in class that no matter how late a person was out on a given night, or how many bars he visited before sleeping in his car, if he faithfully followed the methodological formulas of chemistry, he could achieve the same results repeatedly without risk. Despite threats to the contrary, no students were ever harmed in his presence. The immutable laws of science, Mr. K. proclaimed, are all powerful, as they have a consistency beyond everything known to man.

But life is larger than science. What we want in life is more complex than what can be achieved by mixing smelly powders or dropping Mentos into large bottles of Diet Coke (do try this, but do it outside).[1] And unlike school assignments, we don't want the same results every time. To innovate is to make something new, and progressive science—the discovery of knowledge—is a far cry from what went on in Mr. K.'s classroom. A true experiment has at least one variable that is unknown, and the experiment is to see how that variable, well, varies. What happens if you juggle magnetized bowling balls under water or deep fry a sack of Twinkies in space? If no one knows for certain, you have an experiment on your hands.

While it's one thing to come up with a new idea, a second to try it out and see how it works, it's a less interesting third to follow safe, well-practiced instructions that someone—perhaps a pyromaniac teacher—has laid out for you. Real experiments have risks, just like real life: consider Marie Curie, who discovered radiation but died from it, or the millions of lab rats put out of their cheesy misery every year in the name of exploring new ideas. Innovating comes at a price: it might be money, time, sanity, friends, or marriages, but there will definitely be one.

The myth of methodology, in short form, is the belief that a playbook exists for innovation and, like Mr. K.'s deceptively quaint instructions, it removes risk from the process of finding new ideas. It's the same wish that fuels secret lusts for timesaving gadgets, tasty but low-fat meals (ha), and five-step programs for <insert problem here>. And like other myths, this fantasy sells faster than truth, explaining the films, novels, and infomercials that play on it.

---

[1] *http://eepybird.com/dcm1.html.*

But in our better minds, the one disappointingly easy to fool out of its credit card numbers, we know the *im*possible never happens. We know it's not called the *if-you're-lucky*-possible or the *if-you-read-a-fancy-book-it-may-work*-possible for good reason. There is no way to avoid all risks when doing new things. It takes resources to start a company, develop an idea, or even change someone's mind, and those investments have no guaranteed returns. Even the scientific method, the process behind the ubiquitous "rocket science," doesn't promise success—consider the *Apollo 13* mission or the *Challenger* space shuttle. And methods created by gurus or famous executives all fall well short of predictive; the greatest innovators in history all have more failures in their records than successes. There is good advice to be found, but it's a far cry from methodology.

How innovations start

The top question famed innovators hear is, "How did you start?" It's the beginnings that drive our curiosity: when did Edison get the idea for the lightbulb, or how did the Google founders envision a better search engine? Everyone wants to know where the magic happened, and since they can't imagine the magic sprinkled across years of work, they assume it's a secret—a tangible, singular element hiding behind the start. Like our endless quest to explain the origins of things, we're prone to seeking magic in beginnings.

It's this desire that leads otherwise bright minds to research Michael Jordan's breakfast, da Vinci's or Einstein's napping habits, or Linus Torvalds' (founder of Linux) chosen style of underwear.[2] The irrelevance of these details is obvious here in the logical confines of this book, but we've all considered similarly ridiculous questions about someone we admire. I once researched which typewriter Hemingway had and which inks Shakespeare used to pen his plays. Dreams don't run on logic: when we follow our emotions, we find both amazing and ridiculous things, and it takes time to sort one from the other.

---

[2] I don't know what kind of underwear Linus wears, but my guess is he goes commando: *http://en.wikipedia.org/wiki/Linus_Torvalds*.

The eventual problem with excessive, dreamy curiosity is that—
instead of making our own beginnings, right here and now—we
seek to reuse others' magic, borrowing their beginnings, retrofit-
ting them into our lives.[3] Of course, still safe in this book, we
know details from others' experiences are unlikely to be pivotal in
our own—what worked for them, during their era, won't necessarily work for anyone else. For example, imagine that Alexander
the Great was born in Iceland or Steve Jobs in medieval France—
how well would their "magic" work? There are countless factors
in any success story, and only some belong to the innovators.

Bo Peabody, venture capitalist and founder of Tripod (the eighth
largest web site in 1998) wrote, "Luck is a part of life, and every-
body, at one point or another, gets lucky. But luck is a big part of
business life and perhaps the biggest part of entrepreneurial life."[4]
Acknowledging the uncontrollable factors helps divorce us from
worshiping the details of heroes' achievements. Studying history
grants power, but only when we overcome romance and see innovators as humans just like us with similar limitations and circum-
stantial influences.

The best advice I've read on starting creative work comes from
John Cage, the most innovative composer of the 20th century, who
said, "It doesn't matter where you start, as long as you start."[5] He
meant that there can be no perfect beginning: it's only after you
start—no matter how roughly—that you can evaluate and build
on what you've done, shift directions, or start over with the
insight and perspective you've gained in the process. Innovation is
best compared to exploration, and like Magellan or Captain
Cook, you can't find something new if you limit your travels to
places others have already found.

---

3 "Until one is committed, there is hesitancy, the chance to draw back—Concerning
   all acts of initiative (and creation), there is one elementary truth that ignorance of
   which kills countless ideas and splendid plans: that the moment one definitely
   commits oneself, then Providence moves, too. All sorts of things occur to help one
   that would never otherwise have occurred. A whole stream of events issues from
   the decision, raising in one's favor all manner of unforeseen incidents and meetings and material assistance, which no man could have dreamed would have come
   his way. Whatever you can do, or dream you can do, begin it. Boldness has genius,
   power, and magic in it. Begin it now." —Goethe

4 Bo Peabody, *Lucky or Smart* (Random House, 2004).

5 *http://en.wikipedia.org/wiki/John_Cage*.

The seeds of innovation

The clichés about beginnings are true. The history of innovation is large enough that all the sayings, from Plato's famous "Necessity is the mother of invention" to Emerson's "Build a better mousetrap and the world will beat a path to your door" hold some truth.[6] The trap, and the myth, is that evidence supporting one claim doesn't mean there isn't equally good evidence supporting another. Invention, and innovation, have many parents: the Taj Mahal (Figure 3-2) was built out of sorrow, the Babylonian Gardens were designed out of love,[7] the Empire State Building was constructed for ego, and the Brooklyn Bridge was motivated by pride. Name an emotion, motivation, or situation, and you'll find an innovation somewhere that it seeded.

Figure 3-2. Constructing the Taj Mahal required several innovations, all inspired by an emperor's sadness for his deceased wife.

However, it's simplifying and inspiring to categorize how things begin. In reading the stories behind hundreds of innovations, some patterns surface, and they're captured here in six categories. I

---

6 We'll see in Chapter 8 that Emerson probably never said this.

7 The Babylonian Gardens are a disputed entry in the Seven Wonders of the World; they may never have existed: *http://ancienthistory.suite101.com/article.cfm/the_hanging_gardens_of_babylon.*

concede to the existence of reasonable arguments for seven or five, or different categorizations altogether. I offer this list to seed your thoughts on what paths to innovation are in front of you now.

Hard work in a specific direction

The majority of innovations come from dedicated people in a field working hard to solve a well-defined problem. It's not sexy, and it won't be in any major motion pictures anytime soon, but it's the truth. Their starts are ordinary: in the cases of DNA (Watson and Crick), Google (Page and Brin), and the computer mouse (Englebart), the innovators spent time framing the problem, enumerating possible solutions, and then began experimenting. Similar tales can be found in the origins of the developments of television (Farnsworth) and cell phones (Cooper).[8] Often, hard work extends for years. It took Carlson, the inventor of the photocopier, decades of concentrated effort before Xerox released its first copying machine.[9]

Hard work with direction change

Many innovations start in the same way as mentioned previously, but an unexpected opportunity emerges and is pursued midway through the work. In the classic tale of Post-it Notes, Art Fry at 3M unintentionally created weak glue, but he didn't just throw it away. Instead, he wondered: what might this be good for? For years he kept that glue around, periodically asking friends and colleagues whether it could be useful. Years later, he found a friend who desired sticky paper for his music notations, giving birth to Post-it Notes. Teflon (a mechanical lubricant), tea bags (first used as packaging for loose tea samples), and microwaves (unexpected discharge from a radar system) all have similar origination stories. What's ignored is that the supposed "accident" was made possible by hard work and persistence, and it wouldn't have otherwise happened by waiting around.

---

[8] Singular inventorship is exceptionally rare, as we'll discuss in Chapter 5. For all of these innovations, others rightfully claim partial credit. Several books have been written on the history of television, and it's one of the most complex and distributed stories of innovation in the 20th century.

[9] *http://www.invent.org/hall_of_fame/27.html.*

Curiosity

Many innovations begin with bright minds following their personal interests. The ambition is to pass time, learn something new, or have fun. At some point, the idea of a practical purpose arises, commitments are made, and the rest is history. George de Mestral invented Velcro in response to the burrs he found on his clothes after a hike. He was curious about how the burrs stuck, put them under a microscope, and did some experiments. Like da Vinci, he found inspiration in the natural world, and he designed Velcro based on the interlocking hooks and loops of the burrs and his clothing. Linus Torvalds began Linux as a hobby: a way to learn about software and explore making some of his own.[10] Much like the direction-change scenario, at some point, a possible use is found for the product of curiosity, and a choice is made to pursue it or follow curiosity elsewhere.

Wealth and money

Many innovations are driven by the quest for cash. Peter Drucker believed Thomas Edison's primary ambition was to be a captain of industry, not an innovator: "His real ambition...was to be a business builder and to become a tycoon."[11] Drucker also explains that Edison was a disaster in business matters, but that his profile was so prominent that—despite his entrepreneurial failures—his management methods are emulated today, particularly in Silicon Valley and venture capital firms.

With half an innovation in hand, ideas but no product, it's natural to try to sell those ideas: let someone else take the risks of complete innovation. Instead of idealistic goals of revolution or changing the world, the focus is on reaping financial rewards without the uncertainties of bringing the ideas all the way to fruition. The Internet boom and bust of the 1990s was driven by start-up firms innovating, or pretending to innovate, just enough for established corporations to acquire them. In many cases, the start-ups imploded before acquisition or were acquired only for

---

[10] *http://www.redhat.com/docs/manuals/linux/RHL-6.2-Manual/getting-started-guide/ch-history.html.*

[11] From *Innovation and Entrepreneurship*, 13.

their ideas to be abandoned by the corporations' larger and conservative business plans.

The founders of many great companies initially planned to sell their ideas to larger corporations but, unable to sell, reluctantly chose to go it alone. Google tried to sell to Yahoo! and AltaVista, Apple to HP and Atari, and Carlson (photocopier) to nearly every corporation he could find.

Necessity

Waves of innovation have come from individuals in need of something they couldn't find. Craig Newmark, founder of Craiglist.org, needed a way to keep in touch with friends about local events. The simple email list grew too popular to manage and evolved into the web site known today. Similarly, the founders of McDonald's developed a system for fast food production to simplify the management of their local homespun hamburger stand (Ray Crok bought the company later and developed it into a multinational brand). Innovations that change the world often begin with humble aspirations.

Combination

Most innovations involve many factors, and it's daft to isolate one above others. Imagine an innovation that starts with curiosity and leads to hard work, but then the innovator's quest for wealth forces a direction change. Midway through, this direction change is interrupted by a stroke of good luck (say, winning the lottery), allowing the innovator to return to the initial direction with renewed perspective and motivation. The removal of any of those seeds from the story might end it—or might not. In many of the stories of innovation, we have to wonder: if the first "magical" event didn't take place, might the innovator have found a different seed instead? No matter what seeds are involved, all ideas overcome similar challenges, and studying them reveals as much or more than the beginnings of innovation.

The challenges of innovation

Steve Jobs, founder of Apple and Pixar, was asked, "How do you systematize innovation?" (a common question among CEOs and the business community). His answer was, "You don't."[12] This was not what readers of *Business Week* expected to hear, but foolish questions often receive disappointing answers. It's as absurd a question as asking how to control weather or herd cats, because those approximate the lack of control and number of variables inherent in innovation. Jobs, or any CEO, might have a system for *trying* to manage innovation, or a *strategy* for managing the risks of new ideas, but that's a far cry from systematizing something. I wouldn't call anything with a 50% failure rate a system, would you? The Boeing 777 has jet engines engineered for guaranteed 99.99% reliability—now that's a system and a methodology. It's true that innovation is riskier than engineering, but that doesn't mean we should use words like system, control, or process so casually.

A better question, one with useful answers, is: what challenges do innovations face? While success is unpredictable, the challenges can be identified and used as excellent tools. Any successful innovation can be studied for how those challenges were overcome, and any innovation in progress can be managed with those challenges in mind.

In this chapter's second swoop through the innovations of all time, I've categorized the eight challenges innovations confront.

1. **Find an idea.** Ideas can come from anywhere: concentrated thinking, daydreaming, personal problems, observations of others, a coincidence, or the result of studying something in the world (see Chapter 6). The idea could be for a problem you want to solve or merely for an experiment you want to follow (hoping the problem it solves will surface later—a scenario often mocked as a "solution in search of a problem").

2. **Develop a solution.** The idea is one thing; a working solution is another. Leonardo da Vinci sketched a helicopter in the 1500s, but it would be centuries before developments in aerodynamics and engines would make even a working prototype

---

[12] *http://www.businessweek.com/magazine/content/04_41/b3903408.htm.*

possible. Execution demands more effort than idea generation, and it's difficult to know how much more until you try.
When developing something new, technologies, bank accounts,
and people all have a surprising tendency to disappoint, sending humbled innovators back for variations of challenge #1:
many smaller ideas need to be found to enable the big idea.
Or, the idea is narrowed to make development possible.

3. **Sponsorship and Funding.** How will you fund the project,
including #2? If you work for someone else, you'll need permission or political influence. The management of innovation—in an MBA sense—is finding, managing, and satisfying
sponsors, or positioning an innovation within their political
climate and objectives. If you're independent, you'll need
investors or bank loans, and you must complete enough of #2
to convince them you're worthy of their support.

4. **Reproduction.** It's difficult to scale something: you might
design a better mousetrap, but can you manufacture 50,000
cheaply enough to profit? It's a different challenge to make
thousands of something than it is to make one. Software and
new technologies are appealing to innovators because they ease
many reproduction challenges (DVDs are cheap to reproduce,
as are web sites or servers), but they face issues of scale: having enough bandwidth, speed, or services to satisfy customers.

5. **Reach your potential customer.** An idea is not an innovation
until it reaches people. Some trivialize this by calling it marketing, but the truth is that many innovations fail because
they never reach the people they're designed for. Great innovations have been lost for decades, recovered only when
someone found a way to bring them to the right people. The
wheel, the steam engine, and freeze-dried foods were innovations that existed before 100 BCE, but it took centuries for
innovators to position each of them in ways the average person could use. *Lost Discoveries*, by Dick Teresi, details dozens
of innovations lost to civilization for generations—failures of
marketing and communication more so than technology.

6. **Beat your competitors.** While you're working hard at #1–5, you won't be alone. Steve Jobs (Apple) was not the only maker of personal computers. Bill Gates (Microsoft) did not have the only operating system. Jeff Bezos (Amazon.com) did not have the first online bookstore. The opportunity seen by every successful innovator is visible to others, and those who succeed always leave competitors in their wake. Every breakthrough, at any time, is chased by dozens of talented and motivated people—the wise innovator keeps an eye on his peers' work for purposes of collaboration, inspiration, or tactical recognizance.

7. **Timing.** As great as your idea is, will the culture be ready when it's finished? Revolutionary ideas can be too much change for people to handle. Innovations often need to be explained in terms of the status quo, which is why automobiles are rated in horsepower and electric lights in candles. The risk is that a sufficiently advanced idea, regardless of how it's positioned, won't match the interests or concerns of the moment. Timing is also a factor: what news will break on the day you announce your innovation? What components needed to finish your innovation are delivered late? What will other players and competitors do on the day you launch?

8. **Keep the lights on.** While you're dealing with all the innovation fun above, the bills will keep coming. Being an innovator doesn't give you a "get out of other obligations free" card.

The infinite paths of innovation

The good news that arises from all of these challenges is that there are many ways to succeed. We're lucky: all the great things civilization has created did happen, despite all the reasons they didn't have to. However, which paths are open or closed at any moment is impossible to know. The path that worked last week is not guaranteed to work today, and an innovation that has failed in the past might just be the right thing for right now. Successful innovations are highly unpredictable, even in the view of experts or the innovator themselves, as is the case of three unlikely but telling success stories: 3M, Craigslist, and Flickr.

In the summer of 2002, a small team of Vancouver programmers were working to build an online game called *Game Neverending*. The idea was to build an experience so fun and interesting that people would pay money to spend time in this invented world (similar to today's popular and addictive *World of Warcraft*). One goal the programmers had was to make communication easy between people inside the game, easier even than being in the same room. They built a simple tool that allowed players to talk, exchange instant messages, and share photos. It was a minor part of a major project and, at the time, not much was thought of it.

As weeks passed, they realized the photo-sharing tool they'd built was a more promising business than the game itself. It was fun to use, and as it was improved, it developed features that even professional photo-sharing tools didn't have. With the game incomplete, and their 2002 post-boom tech-sector financing running thin, they strapped on their seatbelts and changed direction. In 2003, it launched under the name Flickr and quickly found a following. Since Flickr's design wasn't nurtured under the scrutiny of a business model, they delivered higher-quality service to customers with ideas none of the existing competitors had ever thought to do. As Fake, one of Flickr's founders, commented, "Had we sat down and said, 'Let's start a photo application,' we would have failed."[13] Because they had the freedom to design a photo application without the same constraints, they were able to design something unique. While Flickr itself probably never made a profit, their technology, design, and loyal customers were attractive enough for Yahoo! to purchase them—even though Yahoo! had its own photo-sharing service.

The folks at Flickr did two key things. First, they recognized the unexpected value of the photo tool. And second, they were willing to make big changes and reinvest everything in a different direction. The paradox is that the opportunity to do these two things presented itself in the course of doing something else: making a computer game. No methodology could guide someone in determining, in the moment, when to abandon one direction and reinvest in another. It is possible that, had they continued with the

---

[13] *http://www.usatoday.com/tech/products/2006-02-27-flickr_x.htm.*

game, it would have been successful, and I'd be writing about the game in this book, instead of Flickr.

It's easy to find similar stories of "innovation by curious path." Today, Google is well known for their rule of giving employees 20% of work time for their own projects, hoping to inspire Flickr-esque innovations. But Google is far from the first company to offer this kind incentive. 3M, the giant products company, began the practice of employee-chosen projects decades earlier, and their success is a great story on its own.

3M started as Minnesota Mining and Manufacturing Co. in 1902, drilling underground for mineral deposits used to make grinding-wheels: a most unexpected beginning for the future makers of cute yellow Post-it Notes.[14] It took 15 years for the struggling company to post profits, mostly with their line of quality sandpaper. Then in 1925, Richard G. Drew, a lab assistant, needed a transparent way to mark borders on objects: namely, automobiles scheduled for two-tone paint jobs.[15] After some experimentation on his own time, masking tape was born, and the history of 3M was changed forever.[16] William McKnight, 3M's general manger, learned from Drew that innovation comes from the bottom where exploration happens; under his leadership, they developed a culture that supports mavericks and experimenters, explaining their amazing $20 billion in annual sales.[17]

One last path to innovation started in 1995 at the dawn of the Internet Age. Craig Newmark, a software engineer in San Francisco, wanted a way to exchange information with friends about cool events happening around his hometown.[18] At first he used email, but soon there was enough traffic that an email list was needed so people could post and reply without annoying each other. At the time, there were many commercial services for this

---

[14] *http://solutions.3m.com/wps/portal/3M/en_US/About/3M/.*

[15] *http://web.mit.edu/invent/iow/drew.html.*

[16] According to legend, prototypes of the tape failed so miserably that Drew was scolded, told to take his tape back to his Scotch bosses, and put more adhesive on it. He kept the name, and Scotch tape was how the product was marketed.

[17] William McKnight captured his philosophy well in a speech given in 1948, summing up in three paragraphs a set of simple ideals modern managers rarely have the courage to live up to. See *http://www.answers.com/topic/william-l-mcknight.*

[18] *http://www.craigslist.org/about/mission.and.history.html.*

sort of information, from newspapers to newsletters to community bulletin boards, but something about the informal and profitless ambitions made it a popular alternative. In 1997, Craig formalized the noncommercial nature of the list, preferring to protect its authenticity and simplicity. It wasn't until 1999 that Craig decided to make Cragislist.org the focus of his working life. Today, the list is one of the most effective job posting and community building web sites in San Francisco and other major U.S. cities.

Had you rounded up all of the great innovation experts and authors from these times, none of them would have predicted these outcomes. In all three cases, common sense would have dictated that the markets involved (photo software, office products, and classified ads) were highly saturated businesses with few opportunities. But now, looking back (as we learned in Chapter 2), it seems inevitable that these markets were ripe for change.

The probability of innovation

As a back-of-the-envelope sketch of innovation difficulty, let's assume there is a 50% chance of succeeding at each challenge (which, given the data, is generous). Because success at one challenge is dependent on the previous, the probability of overcoming all challenges is low:

$$50\% \times 50\% \times 50\% \times 50\% \times 50\% \times 50\% \times 50\% \times 50\% = .390625\%$$

That's less than 1%. Of course, if your innovation requires only convincing your friends to try a new poker variation, or your boss to run meetings differently, you might face two (and not all eight challenges), and odds improve based on your skills, experience, and teammates. It's safe to say that the smaller the ambition, the better the odds. But dreams and passions, the saving throw against probability, might fade.[1] And, as Han Solo said, "Never tell me the odds."[2]

---

[1] Saving throw is a term from role-playing games, where a character has a certain percent chance, influenced by their talents or magic powers, of avoiding nasty things. See *http://en.wikipedia.org/wiki/Saving_throw*.

[2] *http://imdb.com/title/tt0080684/quotes*.

Finding paths of innovation

While there are no maps, there are attitudes that help. Any good survival training course teaches not just skills, but ways to think. The comparison between innovation and survival is apt; to follow the comparison, here are ways of thinking about paths that can shift the odds.

- **Self-knowledge.** Every tough decision is made in part by how the innovator feels about herself: none of us is as logical as we like to believe. Being aware of the environments or challenges that inspire the best results for your personality helps you make smart path choices. The best business opportunity might be the least interesting personal challenge, and vice versa. Knowing yourself, and your team, is a big advantage and should guide decisions. It's one of the few uncertainties of innovation that, given time, can always be converted into certain knowledge and used as an asset.

- **Be intense, but step back.** Many successful innovators work passionately, but periodically step back and ask, "What is happening in the world that impacts my goals?" or "What else is my work good for?" Innovation is powered by the combination of intensity and a willingness to reconsider assumptions, minimizing the chance of following dead ends and maximizing the potential for finding better paths. Honest friends can lend their perspectives if asked—you just have to be ready to hear hard truths. It's difficult to bet years on an idea and maintain the courage to question, rethink, and fully commit again.

- **Grow to size.** No patent was written and filed in an hour, and no symphony was orchestrated overnight. Changing the world or revolutionizing an industry is a nice fantasy, but it's foolish to start with those ambitions because they're out of any individual's control. It makes more sense to attack a specific problem in a known field; only as successes accrue should the ambition grow. Many world-changing ideas had humble beginnings and started with small questions like, "Can I make this better?" Use ego and ambition to fuel a progression of innovations and not to distract you away from the best opportunities, however ordinary, nearby.

- **Honor luck and the past.** The great egos of innovation have one success story that they repeat (to the misery of their companions) forever. Never having the courage to attempt something new or admit the role of luck, they spend much of the present talking about the past. Honoring luck doesn't diminish an accomplishment: it's an acknowledgment to others that you can do everything right and fail, and do many things wrong and succeed. The greatest innovators never failed to acknowledge luck, chance, and the sacrifices of their predecessors. Isaac Newton wrote, "I have stood on the shoulders of giants"[19] and Einstein noted, "Anyone who has never made a mistake has never tried anything new." Perhaps innovators deserve the most respect for their courage in confronting uncertainty, an element common to us all. The bright innovators who failed but refused to quit are more worthy of emulating than the "magic" success stories of those who claim false dominion over things they fear.

---

[19] This quote was almost certainly false modesty. Newton was arrogant and possibly mentally ill, often resorting to childish mockery of his many opponents.

CHAPTER 4

People love new ideas

Imagine it's 1874, and you've just invented the telephone. After hi-fiving your friend Watson, you head down to Western Union—the greatest communication company in the world—and show your work. Despite your excellent pitch (a century before Power-Point), they turn you down on the spot, call the telephone a useless toy, and show you to the door. Would you have given up? What if the next five companies turned you down? The next 25? How long would it take to lose faith in your ideas?

Fortunately, Alexander Graham Bell, the telephone's inventor, didn't listen to the folks at Western Union.[1] He started his own business and changed the world, paving the way for the mobile phone in your pocket. Similar stories surround innovators like Google founders Larry Page and Sergey Brin, whose page rank ideas were turned down by AltaVista and Yahoo!, the dominant search companies of the day. George Lucas was told all kinds of no by every major Hollywood studio but one, for the original *Star Wars* screenplay. And, don't forget that Einstein's $E=mc^2$, Galileo's sun-centered solar system, and Darwin's theory of evolution were laughed at for years by experts around the world.

Every great idea in history has the fat red stamp of rejection on its face. It's hard to see today because once ideas gain acceptance, we gloss over the hard paths they took to get there. If you scratch any innovation's surface, you'll find the scars: they've been roughed up and thrashed around—by both the masses and leading minds—before they made it into your life. Paul C. Lauterbur, winner of the Nobel Prize for coinventing MRI, explained, "you can write the entire history of science in the last 50 years in terms of papers rejected by *Science* or *Nature*."[2] Big ideas in all fields endure dismissals, mockeries, and persecutions (for them and their creators) on their way to changing the world. Many novels in classics libraries, including James Joyce's *Ulysses*, Mark Twain's *The Adventures of Huckleberry Finn*, and J. D. Salinger's *The Catcher*

---

[1] Bell is often credited as the inventor, but Elisha Grey merely failed to file his patent a few hours sooner. Second, Western Union did reject Bell's proposal, but it's unclear how strong their rejection was. (If they saw its potential, would it have been wise to tell Bell on the spot?) See *http://inventors.about.com/library/inventors/bltelephone.htm*.

[2] Kevin Davis, "Public Libraries Open Their Doors," *BIO-IT World*, February 2007, *http://www.bio-itworld.com/archive/111403/plos/*.

in the Rye were banned upon publication; great minds like Socrates and Plato even rejected the idea of books at all.[3]

The love of new ideas is a myth: we prefer ideas only after others have tested them. We confuse truly new ideas with good ideas that have already been proven, which just happen to be new to us. Even innovators themselves read movie reviews, consult Zagat restaurant ratings, and shop at IKEA, distributing the burden of dealing with new ideas. How did you choose your apartment, your beliefs, or even this book? We reuse ideas and opinions all the time, rarely committing to the truly *new*. But we should be proud; it's smart. Why not recycle good ideas and information? Why not take advantage of the conclusions other people have made to efficiently separate what's good and safe from what's bad and dangerous? Innovation is expensive: no one wants to pay the price for ideas that turn out to be not quite ready for prime time.

There is an evolutionary advantage in this fear of new things. Any ancestors who compulsively jumped over every newly discovered cliff or ate only scary looking plants died off quickly. We happily let brave souls like Magellan, Galileo, and Neil Armstrong take intellectual and physical risks on our behalf, watching from a safe distance, following behind (or staying away) once we know the results. Innovators are the test pilots of life, taking big chances so we don't have to. Even early adopters, people who thrive on using the latest things, are at best adventurous consumers, not creators. They rarely take the same risks on unproven ideas as the innovators themselves.

The secret tragedy of innovators is that their desire to improve the world is rarely matched by support from the people they hope to help.

Managing the fears of innovation

What's the most stressful thing that can happen? Juggling hungry cocaine-addicted baby tigers? Doing standup comedy in front of your coworkers and in-laws? Well, if you believe the studies, it's the big five: divorce, marriage, moving, death of a loved one, and getting fired.[4] All stressful events, including tiger juggling, combine

---

3 Plato, *Phaedrus*, *http://classics.mit.edu/Plato/phaedrus.html*.
4 *http://www.surgeongeneral.gov/library/mentalhealth/chapter4/sec1_1.html*.

fear of suffering with forced change. A divorce or new job demands that your life change in ways out of your control, triggering instinctive fears: if you don't do something clever soon, you're going to be miserable (or dead). Although it's possible to endure the big five simultaneously, a notion that quiets most complaints about life, surviving just one devastates most people for months.

Now imagine some relaxing events: reading a funny novel by the ocean or having beers with friends by a midnight campfire. They're activities with little risk and guaranteed rewards. We've done these things many times and know that others have done them successfully and happily in the past. These are the moments we wish we had more of. We work hard so we can maximize the amount of time spent on the planet doing these kinds of things.

Innovation conflicts with this desire. It asks for faith in something unknown over something known to be safe, or even pleasant. A truly innovative Thanksgiving turkey recipe or highway driving technique cannot be risk-free. Whatever improvement it might yield is uncertain the moment it's first tried (or however many attempts are needed to get it right). No matter how amazing an idea is, until proven otherwise, its imagined benefits will pale in comparison to the real, and nonimagined, fear of change.

This creates an unfortunate paradox: the greater the potential of an idea, the harder it is to find anyone willing to try it (more on this in Chapter 8). For example, solutions for world peace and world hunger might be out there, but human nature makes it difficult to attempt them. The bigger the changes needed to adopt an innovation, the more fears rise.

> *There is nothing more difficult to take in*
> *hand, more perilous to conduct, or more*
> *uncertain in its success, than to take the lead*
> *in the introduction of a new order of things.*
> *For the reformer has enemies in all those who*
> *profit by the old order, and only lukewarm*
> *defenders in all those who would profit by the*
> *new order, this lukewarmness arising partly*
> *from fear of their adversaries…and partly*
> *from the incredulity of mankind, who do not*
> *truly believe in anything new until they have*
> *had actual experience of it.*
> —Niccolo Machiavelli

The list of negative things innovators hear

Every creator hears similar criticisms to his ideas. While I don't have proof, I bet the first caveman who captured fire, the first Sumerian with a wheel, the first person to do anything interesting in any society in human history, heard one of the following after he pitched his idea:

- This well never work.
- No one will want this.
- It can't work in practice.
- People won't understand it.
- This isn't a problem.
- This is a problem, but no one cares.
- This is a problem and people care, but it's already solved.
- This is a problem, and people care, but it will never make money.
- This is a solution in search of a problem.
- Get out of my office/cave now.

Sometimes very smart people say these things. Ken Olsen, founder of the Digital Equipment Corporation, said in 1977, "There is no reason anyone would want a computer in their home." The leading art critics in France, in response to the opening of the Eiffel Tower, made comments like, "[that] tragic lamppost springing up from its bowels...[is] like a beacon of disaster and despair."[5] It took the British Navy, at the peak of their dominance in the 17th century, 150 years to adopt a proven remedy for scurvy. Bo Peabody, serial entrepreneur, wrote, "It's astounding the number of people who will tell you and your ideas are crazy. I have been thrown out of more than a thousand offices while building my six companies."[6] Remember, it's hard to know the future, and all great minds have failed to predict what would take off and what wouldn't. My point isn't to make fun of famous people for being wrong; instead, it's to point out that we're all wrong much of the time (see Figure 4-1).

---

[5] John Lienhard, *The Engines of Our Ingenuity* (Oxford University Press, 2006), 186.

[6] From *Lucky or Smart*, 28.

Figure 4-1. Many critics demanded that the Eiffel Tower be torn down when it was built. Today, it's one of Paris' most popular attractions.

Experienced innovators anticipate these criticisms. They prepare refutations or preempt them, as in, "Who would want electricity in their homes? Let me tell you who...."[7] But even with preparation, charm, and amazing ideas, convincing people to see an idea in the same way as its creator is difficult. Most have little interest

[7] Edison was a shameless promoter of electricity, crossing moral and ethical lines. He created the first electric chair to demonstrate that his competitors' designs were unsafe, unlike his (which wasn't true). Matthew Josephson, *Edison: A Biography* (McGraw-Hill, 1959), 348–349.

in having their minds changed, a fact that's hard to remember when you've spent your life savings, or an entire weekend, killing yourself to invent something. This gap—the difference between how an innovator sees his work from how it's seen by others—is the most frustrating challenge innovators face. Creators expect to be well received. They look at accepted innovations and the heroes who delivered them and assume their new innovations will be treated the same way (see Figure 4-2). But no matter how brilliant an idea is, the gap exists. Until the innovation is accepted, it will be questioned relentlessly.

Figure 4-2. *Innovators know of other innovations only after the fact, and they are surprised when their ideas are treated differently from the accepted innovations of the past.*

Many innovators give up when they learn ideas, even with dazzling prototypes or plans in hand, are the beginning. The challenges that follow demand skills of persuasion more than brilliance. As Howard Aiken, a famous inventor, said, "Don't worry about people stealing an idea. If it's original, you will have to ram it down their throats."[8] Although beating up people to convince them rarely works, Aiken's point holds: people are unlikely to be as interested in your ideas as you are.

The observation many would-be innovators never make is that most criticisms are superficial. The spoken questions only hint at the real concerns. Responding to superficial comments is a loser's game, persuading demands mapping criticisms to deeper issues. All of the negative comments listed above can be mapped to one or more of the following perspectives likely held by others:

- **Ego/envy:** I can't accept this because I didn't think of it.
- **Pride and politics:** This makes me look bad.

---

[8] *http://en.wikipedia.org/wiki/Howard_Aiken.*

- **Fear:** I'm afraid of change.
- **Priority:** I have 10 innovative proposals but resources for one.
- **Sloth:** I'm lazy, bored, and don't want to think or do more work.[9]
- **Security:** I may lose something I don't want to lose.
- **Greed:** I can make money or build an empire if I reject this idea.
- **Consistency:** This violates my deeply held principles (no matter how absurd, outdated, or ridiculous they are).

The effect of these feelings, whether justified or irrational, is the same. They're just as real in the mind of the person feeling them as anything else. If your boss feels threatened by a proposal—even if those reasons seem entirely paranoid or delusional to you—those feelings will define his behavior in response to new ideas. If those feelings are strong, it's easy for him to use the comments above to reject proposals for even the greatest ideas. If the innovator defends only the superficial and makes no attempt to persuade the deeper feelings to change, or find ways to recast the innovation so that those feelings become positive, she will fail to get the support she needs.

For example, when Galileo claimed the sun was the center of the solar system, he faced persecution from the Church and the Western world for reasons listed above. It wasn't the idea itself that caused the outrage—it was how that idea made them feel. They didn't care about what was at the center of the solar system. Galileo would have been in similar trouble had he suggested the earth rotated around a purple dragon or a half-eaten sandwich. They weren't upset about the details of his theory; they were angry that anyone would advocate a theory different from the one they believed in (of course, making fun of the Pope didn't help any).[10] It was the principle of the thing and how it questioned their sense of order—two common reasons for rejecting ideas that have nothing to do with the idea itself.

---

9 Related quote: "Most people would rather die than think; in fact, they do so."
   —*Bertrand Russell*

10 In short, when Galileo wrote *Dialogue Concerning the Two Chief World Systems*, he put quotes from Pope Urban VIII into the mouth of his character Simplicius, a fool who is ridiculed for defending against heliocentricism. See James Reston, *Galileo: A Life* (Beard Books, 2000).

This is the magic double-secret principle: innovative ideas are rarely rejected on their merits; they're rejected because of how they make people feel. If you forget people's concerns and feelings when you present an innovation or neglect to understand their perspectives in your design, you're setting yourself up to fail.

The innovator's dilemma explained

Earlier, I asked you to imagine inventing the telephone. Did you like that? Well, you'll like this even more, as this scenario has a surprise ending.

Imagine it's 1851, and you're sick and tired of waiting for the Pony Express to deliver important messages. You happen to meet a Mr. Morse and buy into his idea for using copper wire to send instant messages over great distances. Your friends laugh, telling you to get a real job—wires are silly things for grown men to play with. At great financial risk, you build the first cross country cables in the U.S., and it works, changing the world. Your organization thrives for years; the nation is communicating, for a price, over your cutting-edge digital communication network. Wealthy and famous, attractive people soon throw themselves and their money at you. But you're not finished: in a fit of innovation, you create the first stock ticker in 1866, give the nation its first standardized time service, and revolutionize the financial world with money transfers—allowing people to send cash thousands of miles across the country in seconds.

In the middle of your glory, as your rise to innovation fame reaches untold heights, a young man visits you. He holds an odd machine in his hands. He claims it will replace everything, especially all the things you've struggled all your life to build. He's young, arrogant, and dismissive of your achievements. How long would you listen before you threw a telegraph at him? Could you imagine, given all you'd built, that something as simple as his clunky wooden box would replace everything you know? Or would you have the guts to give up the innovations you'd made and put everything behind the unknown?

This challenge of mind is known as the *innovator's dilemma*. The face off between Western Union and Alexander Graham Bell (dramatized but roughly accurate in my telling) has been played out for centuries, with the captains of one aging innovation protecting their work from the threat of emerging ideas. The concept is well described in Clayton M. Christensen's book, *The Innovator's Dilemma*, which provides hearty business examples of faith in the past blinding smart people from the innovations of the future.[11]

It's both a psychological and economical phenomenon: as people and companies age, they have more to lose. They're not willing to spend years chasing dreams or to endanger what they've worked so hard to build. Attitudes focused on security, risk aversion, and optimization of the status quo eventually become dominant positions, and even become organizational policy at companies that were once young, nimble, and innovative. Even its success enabled it to grow into mainstream businesses, diminishing their interest and capacity for new ideas.

For these reasons, it's rare in art, music, writing, business, and every single creative pursuit for innovators to sustain that role throughout their lives. It's not that their talent wanes, it's more that their interests change. Having succeeded, their strongest desire is not to find new ideas to conquer, but to protect the success they already have.

Frustration + innovation = entrepreneurship?

The last 30 years has seen an amazing wave of innovation at the intersection of technology and entrepreneurship.[12] Companies like Apple, Google, Microsoft, HP, and Yahoo! started as small groups who dismissed the well-worn path of convincing others and chose instead to realize ideas on their own. These start-up ventures were born at the frustration of failing to make innovation happen in larger, established businesses. Had the founders of these companies found positive responses from corporations, history might be different. Frustration with people in power is a

---

[11] Clayton M. Christensen, *The Innovator's Dilemma* (Harvard Business School Press, 2003).

[12] This power combo has been a phenomenon since the early days of the Industrial Revolution, when the first steam engines, factories, and mining systems were pioneered by entrepreneurial technologists, free by modern governments to build businesses on their own. See Arnold Pacey, *The Maze of Ingenuity* (MIT Press, 1992).

perennial complaint among creative minds: Michelangelo and da Vinci were infuriated by their employers' limited ambitions and their peers' conservative natures in the same way creative people are today.[13]

Innovators rarely find support within mainstream organizations, and the same stubbornness that drives them to work on problems others ignore gives them the strength necessary to work alone. This explains the natural bond between breakthrough thinkers and new companies; innovative entrepreneurs not only have the passion for new ideas, but they also have the conviction to make sacrifices that scare established companies.

The risks for an individual focusing 100% of his resources on a crazy idea are small: it's one life. But for an organization of 500 or 10,000 people, the risks of betting large on a new idea are high. Even if the idea pays off, the organization will be forced to change, causing fears and negative emotions to surface from everyone invested in the success of the previous big idea. Of course, some corporations are so large that they can take great risks: they can lose $20 million on an experiment and survive. But these efforts fail so often that it's possible that having less to lose works against innovation, compared to scrappy bootstrapped efforts led by people with everything at stake.

But as rosy as it sounds, the entrepreneur, whether she's wealthy or happy living on ramen noodles,[14] must eventually convince one group of people—customers—of the merit of her ideas. And if she doesn't have enough money to support her new ideas, or her family refuses to eat canned chili for the third straight month, she'll need to convince a second group—investors. As far as we know, both groups are human beings (though some debate the DNA of venture capitalists) and have the same emotional responses listed above.

---

[13] However, the major difference between the 15th century and the present day is opportunity. Back then, if you had an idea for cathedral design or siege weapons (hot technologies of the day), you were dependent on the one organization that could afford your services: the Church. But software programmers in the late 20th century and beyond not only have many patrons, they have the means to build their dreams themselves.

[14] For a trifecta of innovation, see Tadashi Katoh and Akira Imai, *Project X - Nissin Cup Noodle* (Digital Manga Publishing, 2006). It's a graphical novel history of how instant ramen noodles were invented, and how the office staple of noodles in a cup came to be.

How innovations gain adoption (the truth about ideas before their time)

One frequent saying in innovation circles is "an idea ahead of its time." What a strange phrase. How can an idea be ahead of its time? How can anything be ahead of its time? It makes no sense. What people mean when they say this is one of two things: they think the idea is cool but not necessarily good, or they're trying to get you to buy it. But it's a lousy pitch. How often do the things we imagine from the future work out in the present? Personal rocketships? Cars that fly? Nuclear-powered everything? The odds of cool ideas from sci-fi movies gaining adoption are poor, and it's far from a compliment to have something labeled "ahead of its time."[15] People don't slave away on insanely difficult work, sacrificing the pleasures of life, with the singular hope that, on their deathbeds, after everything they've done has been ignored, they will be told they were "ahead of their time." To be told your idea is ahead of its time is innovation pity, not praise.

But more importantly for us, this phrase exposes myths about how innovations do gain adoption in the world. First, it assumes technology progresses in a straight line (as covered in Chapter 2). To be ahead of its time implies than an idea *has* a time, marked in red at the universal innovation headquarters, waiting for people to catch up to it: an entirely inaccurate, innovation-centric view of how people live.

In *Diffusion of Innovations*, Everett M. Rogers writes:

> *Many technologists think that advantageous innovations will sell themselves, that the obvious benefits of a new idea will be widely realized by potential adopters, and that the innovation will therefore diffuse rapidly. Unfortunately, this is very seldom the case. Most innovations in fact diffuse at a surprisingly slow rate.*[16]

The book takes an anthropological approach to innovation, suggesting that new ideas spread at speeds determined by psychology and sociology, not the abstract merits of those new ideas. This explains the mysteries of great innovations that fail and bad ideas

---

15 Notice I said movies, not sci-fi books. Films are visual media and choose technologies that look good or have dramatic value, not necessarily things that solve important problems, have progressive value, or obey the laws of physics.

16 Everett M. Rogers, *Diffusion of Innovations* (Free Press, 2003), 15.

that prevail—there are more significant factors than the ones inventors focus on. Technology prowess matters much less than we think in the diffusion of innovation.

Rogers identifies five factors that define how quickly innovations spread; they belong in every innovator's playbook. Roughly summarized and loosely interpreted, they include:

1. **Relative advantage.** What value does the new thing have compared to the old? This is perceived advantage, determined by the potential consumer of the innovation, not its makers. This makes it possible for a valueless innovation—from the creator's perspective—to gain acceptance, while more valuable ones do not. Perceived advantage is built on factors that include economics, prestige, convenience, fashion, and satisfaction.

2. **Compatibility.** How much effort is required to transition from the current thing to the innovation? If this cost is greater than the relative advantage, most people won't try the innovation. These costs include people's value systems, finances, habits, or personal beliefs. Rogers describes a Peruvian village that rejected the innovation of boiling water because of cultural beliefs that hot foods were only for sick people. You could argue all you wanted about the great benefits of boiling water, but if a religious or cultural belief forbids it, you're wasting your breath. Technological compatibility is only part of what makes an innovation spread: the innovation has to be compatible with habits, beliefs, values, and lifestyles.

3. **Complexity.** How much learning is required to apply the innovation? If a box of free, high-quality, infinite battery-life cell phones (and matching solar-powered cell towers) mysteriously appeared in 9th-century England, usage would stay at 0%, as the innovation requires a jump in complexity that would terrify people ("They're witches' eggs—burn them!"). The smaller the perceived conceptual gap, the higher the rate of acceptance.

4. **Trialability.** How easy is it to try the innovation? Teabags were first used as giveaways so people could sample tea without buying large tins, radically improving the trialability of brewed tea.[17] Samples, giveaways, and demonstrations are

---

[17] Joel Levy, *Really Useful: The Origins of Everyday Things* (Firefly Books Ltd, 2002).

centuries-old techniques for making it risk-free to try new ideas. This is why the GAP lets you try on clothes, and the Honda dealership gives anyone with a pulse a test-drive. The easier it is to try, the faster innovations diffuse.

5. **Observability.** How visible are the results of the innovation? The more visible the perceived advantage, the faster the rate of adoption, especially within social groups. Fashion fads are a great example of highly observable innovations that have little value beyond their observability. Advertising fakes observability, as many ads show people using a product, say, drinking a new brand of beer, with all kinds of wonderful things happening. Many technologies have limited observability, say, software device drivers, compared to physical products like mobile phones and trendy handbags, which people use socially.

This list clarifies why the speed at which innovations spread is determined by factors that are often ignored by innovators. They grow so focused on creating things that they forget that those innovations are good only if people can use them. While there's a lot to be said for raising bars and pushing envelopes, breakthroughs happen for societies when innovations diffuse, not when they remain forever "ahead of their time."

This list is a scorecard for learning from past innovations, as well as a tool for improving diffusion of innovations in the present. The key is to trivialize this list as bastardized marketing, as if these traits can be grafted to an innovation after it's finished, or simply pumped into sales literature and advertising (though those efforts rarely make the difference). Is it a successful innovation if it's purchased but ignored or bought and soon returned? A better way to think of the list is as attributes of the innovation itself.

And since these factors vary from culture to culture, some innovations gain acceptance in surprising ways. There is no uniformity in progress around the world; innovations may be adopted by one culture or nation decades before another. As William Gibson wrote, "The future is here. It's just not widely distributed yet," and no innovation is immune. Everything new passes through groups of people in unpredictable ways and, given the limits of human nature, always will.

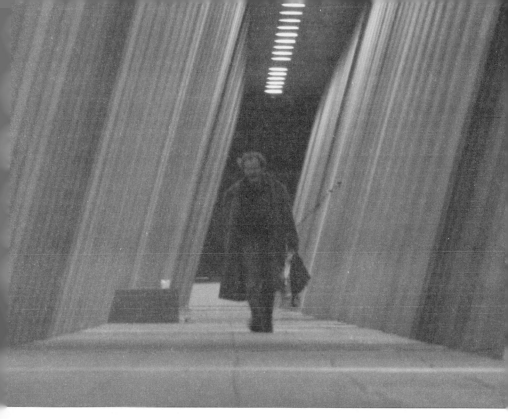

The lone inventor

Who invented the electric light? No, it wasn't Thomas Edison. Two lesser-known inventors, Humphrey Davy and Joseph Swan, both developed working electric lights well before Edison. Think Ford invented the automobile? Wrong again. Unfortunately, popular credit for major innovations isn't brokered by historians: it's driven by markets, circumstance, and popularity, forces not bound by accuracy. Often, even historians have trouble sorting it out. Here's what the U.S. Library of Congress has to say on the subject, specific to the automobile:[1]

> This question [who invented it] does not have a straightforward answer. The history of the automobile is very rich and dates back to the 15th century when Leonardo da Vinci was creating designs and models for transport vehicles. There are many different types of automobiles—steam, electric, and gasoline—as well as countless styles. Exactly who invented the automobile is a matter of opinion. If we had to give credit to one inventor, it would probably be Karl Benz from Germany. Many suggest that he created the first true automobile in 1885/1886.

If the librarians at the largest library in the world don't know, how could we? There are similar complexities surrounding most innovations, from the first steam engines to personal computers or even airplanes (no, it's not the Wright brothers[2]). As simple as it should be, innovation history is complicated. Most innovations are not the solid, tangible, independent things we imagine them to be. Each one is made up of threads and relationships that don't separate easily or yield simple answers.

For example, take the electric light. When Edison sat down to design the lightbulb, he was far from the first person to try. If several people were trying to make it work, who deserves the credit? Would it be enough to come up with the idea itself? Have a prototype? Would it matter how long the prototype stayed alight? How bright it burned? How many people witnessed it? How many bulbs were sold? Would it matter whether they cost $5,000,000 per bulb or weighed 500,000 pounds? Depending on which question is seen

---

[1] http://www.loc.gov/rr/scitech/mysteries/auto.html.

[2] Bet that got you to look at the footnotes. The Wright brothers were first to demonstrate sustained powered flight of a certain distance. But balloons, kites, gliders, and some powered winged vehicles did fly before. More so, the Wright brothers were great researchers and students, learning from birds as well as their competitors. Fred Kelly, *The Wright Brothers* (Dover, 1989).

as most important, different names surface as the rightful owner of the title "inventor." However, as folks at the U.S. Library of Congress suggest, there is no guidebook: the rules change from innovation to innovation. While there is some guidance for resolving these issues, before we get to explore them, things get worse.

Beyond the innovation itself, there is the problem of precedence: various invented light sources date back as far as 70,000 BCE. The idea of a lightbulb, a small portable object that gives light, is beyond ancient—it's older than the screw (500 BCE), the wheel (3000 BCE), and the sword (5000 BCE).[3] The inventors of torches, candles, and lamps through history are mostly unnamed, but they certainly contributed to Swan's, Davy's, and Edison's thinking[4] (not to mention proving to the world the value of being able to easily see the way to the bathroom after sunset). In similar fashion, web sites derive layouts and graphic design techniques from newspapers, which are based on the early typographies of the printing press, and on it goes. All innovations today are bound to innovations of the past.

And if that's not enough, there are the people who developed the glassmaking techniques required for the bulbs, the copper mining and metal refinement processes for the filaments, and countless other forgotten creators of the tools, machines, and mathematics Edison and other innovators used. Certainly their anonymous contributions were essential to the innovation known as the lightbulb: remove them from the past, and in that same puff of history-changing smoke, the electric light we know disappears.

The answer to the list of questions above is simple: Edison, Ford, and countless innovators are recognized as sole inventors for convenience. The histories we know depart from the truth for the simple reason that it makes them easier to remember.

---

[3] It was hard to find hard evidence about the origins of all three of these ancient inventions, so the truth is that we're not really sure. The best single reference on the origins of ancient innovations is *Ancient Inventions* by Peter James and Nick Thorpe (Ballentine Books, 1994).

[4] A concise history can be found at *http://inventors.about.com/library/inventors/bllight.htm*.

The convenience of lone inventors

The most common convenience is order of exposure. Most of the world first learned of the idea of electric lights and lightbulbs from Edison. No matter the actual history, in their knowledge, he was the deliverer of the idea. Even if the world later discovered that others had the idea first, or made working lightbulbs before him, it's natural that people would still remember and use the association with Edison. Whoever is most visible in bringing something new, even if it's only to us, will forever be associated with that thing. Ask any four-year-old who invented love, and odds are high she'll say, "my mom." If we've been exposed to only one source for something, how could we imagine others?

This tendency extends to the names of things. As a kid, I laughed when my grandparents called every refrigerator "Fridgidaire"— the first brand of consumer refrigerator in America (1919)[5]—until I realized I often use brand names, such as Kleenex, Band-Aid, Ziploc, Frisbee, or Post-it Notes, as many people do, in similarly incorrect fashion.[6] Since those were the names I first associated with their respective innovations (tissues, adhesive bandage strips, resealable bags, etc.), they stayed with me. Even though I now know some of them were not the first brand to exist, or when I'm aware I'm using a similar product made by a competitor, I often thoughtlessly use the wrong name.

Ford and Edison paid for marketing campaigns to promote their innovations, businesses, and themselves. As businessmen, they had every reason to promote their work in ways that suggested they deserved every last drop of credit. They became media darlings of their times, appearing in interviews and books, and benefiting— just as star CEOs of today—from the power of public attention. It became convenient for journalists to write in an Edison- or Ford-centric view because making the inventors star characters increased the public's interest in the news.

---

[5] *http://www.history.com/exhibits/modern/fridge.html.*

[6] In 2006, Harris Interactive published a brand study of the product names that have the strongest dominance and recognition for that product line. Other dominant brand names are Heinz (ketchup), Clorox (bleach), and Hershey's (chocolate): *http://www.harrisinteractive.com/news/allnewsbydate.asp?NewsID=1063.*

Innovators became easy heroes in America; people preferred to
believe, and tell, positive stories about them rather than the less
interesting, and more complicated, truths. Would anyone in 1917,
during WWI, have cared to know that the Duryea brothers, and
not Ford, started the first American car company?[7] Or that Ford
owed homage to Leonardo da Vinci, Karl Benz, and others with
strange names from foreign lands? Those details, no matter how
honest, painted a complex and less patriotic story, which writers
on competitive deadlines avoided. The small oversights that were
necessary to cram complex truths into simple hero-shaped tales
were convenient and comfortable for everyone—from newspapers
to journalists to readers and their heroes—and it still happens
today.

One popular example is Apple Inc., well recognized as the innovative company behind the user-friendly Macintosh and the iPod
digital music player. However, history shows that the first products of those types were made by others years earlier. The first
graphical user interfaces, mice, and desktop computers were developed by Xerox PARC and SRI systems in the 1970s, nearly a
decade before Apple's first Macintosh in 1984. The first iPod, sold
in 2001, was late to the game by years—digital music players from
SaeHan, Diamond Multimedia, and Creative labs, using flash
memory and similar core design concepts sold in the late 1990s.
And of course the Sony Walkman, first sold in 1979, was the true
progenitor of the idea of personal, portable music.

Apple, like Edison, earned well-deserved credit for vastly
improving existing ideas, refining them into excellent products,
and developing them into businesses, but Apple did not invent the
graphical user interface, the computer mouse, or the digital music
player. Similarly, Google did not invent the search engine, and
Nintendo did not invent the video game. They deserve credit for
many things, but other companies established the ideas and
proved the concepts behind them. We want innovation explained
in neat packages, but we also want to acclaim the right people for
the right reasons: rarely do both happen simultaneously, unlike
the invention of things themselves.

---

[7] *http://www.loc.gov/rr/scitech/mysteries/auto.html.*

The challenge of simultaneous invention

Have you ever arrived at a party or work to find that someone is wearing the same shirt, pants, or shoes as you? It's a curiosity of modern life that we convince ourselves our wardrobes are unique, despite selecting the items from department stores' racks filled with dozens of the same shirts, slacks, and blouses. An observant shopper watching the goings on at the mall can easily imagine someone—roughly her size—heading home with a similar outfit. Yet if she ever does meet her fashion doppelganger at a party or on the street, she is astonished: "How could *she* wear *my* wardrobe?" Once obtained, regardless of how or why, we take conceptual possession: "That shirt with those pants is my idea."

Fashion is a good metaphor for the problem of simultaneous inventorship: the situation when two or more people claim to have invented something. Like wardrobe collision, it seems improbable in the moment that two people could unintentionally invent the same thing around the same time; stepping back, it's easy to see why it happens. The invention of calculus, television, telephones, bicycles, motion pictures, MRI imaging, and automobiles all involve various kinds of simultaneous, overlapping, or disputed origins.

It's common because innovations demand prerequisite knowledge—inventing a new cocktail (e.g., The Berkun[8]) requires experience with different liquors, and creating a new dance step (e.g., The Edison) demands knowledge of choreography. This narrows the number of people who could create a particular innovation. Add the limited number of popular problems in any field, and suddenly the number of people chasing particular challenges isn't so large.

For example, there are only so many people today working on better word processors, photo-sharing web sites, or email applications. They go to the same industry events, read the same books, and see the same progress among mutual competitors—not to mention the shared experiences that come from being alive at the

---

[8] Nominations for recipes for the drink "The Berkun" can be submitted at *http://www.scottberkun.com/contact*. Entries that include sarcastic ingredients such as "bad writer juice" or "idiot Schnapps" will be disqualified. Winner receives paid vacation to Hawaii (total lie).

same time (and at a good time). In *Creativity in Science*, Dean Simonton explains:

> *Galileo became a great scientist only because he had the fortune of being born in Italy during the time when it became the center of scientific creativity. Similarly, Newton's creative genius could appear only because he lived in Great Britain when the center had shifted there from Italy. If Galileo and Newton had switched birth years without changing national origins, then neither would have secured a place in the annals of science.*[9]

Given the combination of shared factors, odds are reasonable that people in the same field, at the same time, studied in the same universities or learned from the same textbooks. They might even have mutual friends, drinking buddies, or dance partners, making the chances for simultaneous invention unexpectedly high: as free as people are to think creatively, there is a wardrobe of existing ideas that they're all shopping from.

What makes simultaneous invention contentious is that creators often work in isolation from—yet in competition with—their peers, making them prone to fantasies that their creations are unique. In the case of calculus (an innovation that destroyed my college GPA), two brilliant minds made the same conceptual leap, independently: Isaac Newton and Friedrich Leibniz separately developed systems for calculus. In that particular case, the inventions were offset by time, so they weren't technically simultaneous: Newton didn't formally publish his work until 1693; Leibniz published in 1684. Despite their love of reason, things were ugly in the scientific community as debates raged over which man was the rightful inventor—for years England and Germany, Newton's and Leibniz's respective nations, used different versions of calculus, each one claiming righteousness out of national pride.[10]

---

[9] Some believe in the zeitgeist theory of innovation—that cultural forces tell the true story of innovation. How else can we explain the Western Renaissance, Enlightenment, and Dark Ages without looking at the entire environment? From this viewpoint, individuals pay a large debt to factors beyond their control.

[10] In *The Engines of Our Ingenuity*, John Lienhard writes, "That riddle dogs all of science. Equally futile arguments rage over who discovered oxygen. Was it Priestley who first isolated it? Lavoisier, who recognized it as a new substance but failed to identify what the substance was, or Scheele, who got it right before either Priestley or Lavoisier but didn't publish until after they had?"

More recently, the invention of television involved a five-way overlap of creative effort more complex than the Newton/Leibniz debate. Paul Nipkow was the first to consider sending images over wires back in 1884, but he never made a working prototype. In 1907, A. A. Campbell-Swinton and Boris Rosing were the first to suggest cathode ray tubes, but it wasn't until Vladimir Zworkin and Philo Farnsworth—working separately in the 1920s—that true working models of television existed. The inventors worked independently but simultaneously at the same basic goals with trails of overlapping concepts, progressions, and business politics too complex to follow. Like most innovations, if you crack open the invention of television in search of singular answers, you find more questions (which we'll explore later in this chapter).

One solution would be to clarify what it means to be "the inventor." As Brian Dickens, a software engineer explains:

> It is open for question whether "inventor" should suggest the person who came up with the initial idea for an item, the first person to build a working model, or the first person to success-fully commercialize the invention. Obviously, for a new tech-nology to ever make it into practical use, all three of these steps must be taken—but they will never be made all at once by the same individual, with no outside influences.[11]

It's smart advice. The problem is the sizable work involved in sorting out these details. The convenience of collapsing these facts down into a simple story is hard to resist.

The myth of the lone inventor

Everyone knows that Neil Armstrong was the first person on the moon. But how many people helped him get there? Of course there was the rest of the crew: Buzz Aldrin and the oft-forgotten Michael Collins. Then, just like in the movies, there were the dozens of worried-looking mission-control staff on the ground, and notables like Van Braun—intellectual forces who drove the entire program.[12] But what about the people who made the many complicated parts needed to construct *Apollo 11*? And what about

---

11 *http://www.acmi.net.au/AIC/DICKENS.html.*
12 *http://en.wikipedia.org/wiki/Wernher_von_Braun.*

the managers, designers, and planners who conceived the ideas, organized engineering teams, and coordinated years of work? The numbers add up fast. More than 500,000 people worked on the NASA effort to put a person on the moon. For Armstrong to succeed required contributions from an entire metropolis worth of people, not including the millions of taxpayers who paid the bills, and the president who challenged a nation to believe. Neil Armstrong is a household name only because his contribution was the most visible. However, the most visible contribution isn't necessarily the most significant.

The fact that we know the names Neil Armstrong, Leonardo da Vinci, or Frank Lloyd Wright is an innovation all its own. If you want to know who designed the Egyptian pyramids, the Roman Coliseum, or the Great Wall of China, you're out of luck: no one knows. It wasn't until the 1500s and the rise of the Renaissance that Western cultures grew comfortable acknowledging people's creative abilities and individual achievements (we covered this briefly in Chapter 1). Arnold Pacey writes in *The Maze of Ingenuity*, "Creation had previously been thought of as the prerogative of god; now it was seen as activity in which mankind could share...." While the inventors of the compass, the sword, or the mechanical clock missed their chance to make the history books, most inventions since the Renaissance have been credited to one or more individuals.[13] Until then it wasn't important or culturally acceptable to document who deserved credit for creativity.

This shift came with baggage: not everyone was allowed in the special "creative" club. The only people with creative license were geniuses, the Michelangelos and da Vincis, whose talents seemed to stretch beyond human limitations. The rest of us, ordinary as we are, were expected to happily extend our worship to include these superhumans. Yet, these people, for all their brilliance, rarely worked alone. They shared their meals, romances, and daily lives with others, from ordinary shopkeepers to honest craftsmen, who influenced them and their work in many ways. Raphael,

---

[13] The inventors of duct tape are unknown: the rise of corporations has clouded individual credit for many innovations. Johnson & Johnson produced duct tape for the military in 1942. However, duct tape is arguably a modified version of masking tape, invented decades earlier by 3M. If curious about its infinite uses, see *The Jumbo Duct Tape Book*, by Jim Berg and Tim Nyberg (Workman Publishing Company, 2000).

Plato, and Edison all had apprentices (in fact, when they were young, they worked as apprentices to older masters). They studied the great works of their time and had significant aid from unnamed assistants in making their masterpieces. They also benefited from powerful friendships: da Vinci was a pal of Machiavelli; Michelangelo was childhood friends with Pope Clement (who, as an adult, would commission many great works from him).

Rivalries played roles, too: would Michelangelo or da Vinci, motivated by their mutual dislike for each other, have produced the same masterpieces if stranded on separate deserted islands? Michelangelo hated painting, and the Sistine Chapel was likely motivated in part to show up da Vinci. Would Coke be the company it is today without Pepsi? Microsoft without Apple? Take the supporting factors away, and the supposedly sole innovator doesn't seem superhuman anymore.

To be fair, those innovators are still amazing and awesome in their own right. Replacing Michelangelo with Britney Spears, or Edison with my dog Max—while leaving all other forces intact— would produce zero masterpieces (though Max is pretty smart). But the work of these individuals was far from solo or divine. If you look hard, you can find rare individuals who do achieve greatness in isolation—Tesla and Newton were notorious loners— but they are so rare, and their behavior so eccentric, that they are tough examples to learn from.

Today, years away from the Renaissance, we're still attached to the myth of lone inventors. We do recognize collaboration and partnerships, but we often fall back on tales of lone innovators as heroic figures for reasons of convenience. We insist on isolating credit and dismissing the importance of others. Patent law, by design, credits one or a handful of individuals, assuming not only that ideas are unique and separable, which is dubious, but that individual names can be given legal ownership of ideas. Patents, as currently applied in the U.S., do solve problems, but they create just as many. They distort popular understanding of how inventions happen, as well as which innovations are most valuable to the world.[14]

---

[14] For example, 1 in 5 people in the world doesn't have clean drinking water, and 1 in 4 doesn't have reliable electricity. Few patents filed this year will be of use to them. See *http://news.bbc.co.uk/2/hi/science/nature/755497.stm*.

Guy Kawasaki, author of *Rules for Revolutionaries* and former Apple fellow, argues for demystifying lone invention. In his experience, great innovations, and businesses, are born when two or more creators work together to make things happen. He recommends:

> *Find a few soulmates. History loves the notion of the sole innovator: Thomas Edison (lightbulb), Steve Jobs (Macintosh), Henry Ford (Model T), Anita Roddick (The Body Shop), Richard Branson (Virgin Airlines). History is wrong. Successful companies are started, and made successful by at least two, and usually more, soulmates. After the fact one person may come to be recognized as "the innovator," but it always takes a team of good people to make any venture work.[15]*

Grand partnerships are easy to find: John Lennon and Paul McCartney, W. S. Gilbert and Arthur Sullivan, Bill Gates and Paul Allen, and Larry Page and Sergey Brin.

Stepping stones: the origins of spreadsheets and $E=mc^2$

When new TVs or mobile phones sit on store shelves, they seem self-contained. The experience is designed to inspire awe: innovations are placed on shrine-like displays with no signs of their manufacturing; all finished, polished, and gift-wrapped in plastic; waiting to be taken home. But if you look under the cover of any innovation, the magic of self-containment fades. There are subinventions, subproducts, minor-breakthroughs, and parts and components, each with a story of their own. Every wondrous thing is comprised of many other wondrous things.

In *The Engines of Our Ingenuity*, John Lienhard writes:

> *The smallest component of any device, something so small as a screw, represents a long train of invention. Somebody conceived of a lever, someone else thought of a ramp, and another person dreamed up a circular staircase. The simple screw thread merges all of those ideas, and it followed all of them...each part represents a skein of invention, and the whole is a device that we would normally not see in the parts alone.*

15 Guy Kawasaki, *The Art of the Start: The Time-Tested, Battle-Hardened Guide for Anyone Starting Anything* (Portfolio, 2004), 10.

Mobile phones and DVD players have dozens of screws—not to mention transistors, chips, batteries, and software. Take any of those pieces, divide again, and there's even more innovation hiding inside. It's easy to forget that the innovations we use are comprised of a series of smaller innovations. However, making new things requires taking apart other things and learning from the pieces. Sometimes inventors even work the other way, developing breakthroughs by deliberately experimenting with existing innovations.

The first killer app, the software that legitimized personal computers, was the spreadsheet.[16] Before VisiCalc was released for the Apple II in 1978, most of the world did budgets, accounting, and business planning on paper.[17] VisiCalc was the reason computers shifted from geek toys to mainstream business problem-solving tools. Dan Bricklin, one of the creators of VisiCalc, developed the idea while pursuing an MBA at Harvard. In his mind, the birth of VisiCalc came from a combination of existing ideas (count the previous innovations he mentions in this short passage):

> I would daydream. "Imagine if my calculator had a ball in its back, like a mouse..." (I had seen a mouse previously, I think in a demonstration at a conference by Doug Engelbart, and maybe the Alto) "...imagine if I had a heads-up display, like in a fighter plane, where I could see the virtual image hanging in the air in front of me. I could just move my mouse/keyboard calculator around, punch in a few numbers, circle them to get a sum, do some calculations, and answer '10% will be fine!'"[18]

His early vision for VisiCalc involved calculators, mice, fighter planes, the paper spreadsheets he'd seen in his MBA classes, his frustrations with boring accounting assignments, and his awareness of what a computer programming language might be able to build. Naturally, as VisiCalc developed, the dependence on these ideas faded. Bricklin explains, "Eventually, my vision became

---

16 Killer app, or killer application, is a name given to the first software on any computer that drives purchasing of the computer itself. See *http://en.wikipedia.org/wiki/Killer_application*.

17 For entertainment and historical purposes, you can download a PC version of the original VisiCalc. It's useful if ever you forget how far we've come. See *http://www.danbricklin.com/history/vcexecutable.htm*.

18 *http://www.bricklin.com/history/saiidea.htm*.

more realistic, and the heads-up display gave way to a normal screen. The mouse was replaced in the first prototype in the early fall of 1978 by the game paddle of the Apple II." However, those ideas remained building blocks and inspirations. Remove one and VisiCalc may not have been made.

This theme of connections isn't limited to technology: you can find similar webs of innovation in all fields, from business to the arts to science. James Burke's famous book *Connections*[19] relentlessly explores the intertwined nature of inventions. Even the most famous five characters in the world, E=mc^2, credited to Einstein, were based on concepts that came from many people. In David Bodanis' book, *E=mc^2*,[20] he explains how the work of Faraday, Lavoisier, Newton, and Galileo were the essential building blocks that made Einstein's formula possible. Each contribution—*E* for energy, *m* for mass, and *c* for the speed of light—was a concept developed by others; Einstein's breakthrough was his approach in bringing them all together.

Despite the myths, innovations rarely involve someone working alone, and never in history has an invention been made without reusing ideas from the past. For all of our chronocentric glee, our newest ideas have historic roots: the term *network* is 500 years old, webs were around before the human race, and the algorithmic DNA is more elegant and powerful than any programming language. Wise innovators—driven by passion more than ego—initiate partnerships, collaborations, and humble studies of the past, raising their odds against the timeless challenges of innovation.

---

[19] James Burke, *Connections* (Little, Brown and Company, 1978).

[20] David Bodanis, *E=mc^2: A Biography of the World's Most Famous Equation* (Berkeley Trade, 2001).

CHAPTER 6

Good ideas are hard to find

While waiting in a city park to interview someone for this book, a nearby child played with Silly Putty and Legos at the same time. In my notepad I listed how many ideas the young boy, not more than five years old, came up with in 10 minutes. Sitting in the grass, he combined, modified, enhanced, tore apart, chewed on, licked, and buried various creations I'd never have imagined. His young mother, chatting on a phone while resting her morning coffee on the park bench, barely noticed the inventive creations her toddler unleashed on the world. After being chased away for making her nervous (an occupational risk of writers in parks), I wondered what happens to us, and what will happen to this boy, in adulthood. Why, as is popularly believed, do our creativity abilities decline, making ideas harder to find? Why aren't our conference rooms and board meetings as vibrant as childhood playgrounds and sandboxes?

If you ask psychologists and creativity researchers, they'll tell you that it's a myth: humans, young and old, are built for creative thinking. We've yet to find special creativity brain cells that die when you hit 35, or special hidden organs born only to the gifted that pass ideas to our minds. Many experts even discount genius, claiming that the amazing creations by Mozart or Picasso, for example, created their amazing works through ordinary means, exercising similar thinking processes to what we use to escape shopping mall parking lot mazes or improvise excuses when late for dinner.[1] Much like children, the people who earn the label *creative* are, as Howard Gardner explains in *Frames of Mind*,[2] "not bothered by inconsistencies, departures from convention, non-literalness...", and run with unusual ideas that most adults are too rigid, too arrogant, or too afraid to entertain.

The difference between creatives and others is more attitude and experience than nature. We survived hundreds of thousands of years not because of our sharp claws, teleportive talents, or regenerative limbs, but because our oversized brains adapt, adopt, and make use of what we have. If we weren't naturally creative and couldn't find ideas, humans would have died out long ago. A sufficiently motivated bear or lion can easily kill any man—even the

---

[1] Robert W. Weisberg, *Creativity: Beyond the Myth of Genius* (W. H. Freeman, 1993).

[2] Howard Gardner, *Frames of Mind: The Theory of Multiple Intelligences* (Basic Books, 1993).

scariest, meanest, all-pro NFL linebacker. However, given creative problems to solve, an average human being is hard to beat. We make tools, split atoms, and have more patents than the world's species' combined (but please don't tell the bears—they get pissy about patents). Our unique advantage on this planet is the inventive capacity of our minds. We even make tools for thought, like writing, so that when we find good ideas—such as how to tame and cage lions—we can pass that knowledge to future generations, giving them a head start.

But with the advance of civilization, creativity has moved to the sidelines. Idea reuse is so easy—in the form of products, machines, web sites, and services—that people go for years without finding ideas on their own. Modern businesses thrive on selling prepackaged meals, wardrobes, holidays, entertainments, and experiences, tempting people to buy convenience rather than make things themselves.[3] The need for craftsmen and artists, professional idea finders, has faded; more people than ever make livings in careers Lloyd Dobler would hate: selling, buying, and processing other things.[4] Even when charged to work with ideas, few adults can do so as easily as they could in their youth.

Einstein said "imagination is more important than knowledge," but you'd be hard-pressed to find schools or corporations that invest in people with those priorities. The systems of education and professional life, similar by design, push the idea-finding secrets of fun and play to the corners of our minds, training us out of our creativity.[5] We reward conformance of mind, not independent thought, in our systems—from school to college to the workplace to the home—yet we wonder why so few are willing to take creative risks. The truth is that we all have innate skills for solving problems and finding ideas: we've just lost our way.

---

3 My position is not that everyone should make everything themselves, but that 1) everyone has the capacity to enjoy creating something, and 2) the temptation for convenience prevents many people from discovering what it is they like to make.

4 Llyod Dobler is the main character of the film *Say Anything*, played by John Cusack. "I don't want to sell anything, buy anything, or process anything as a career. I don't want to sell anything bought or processed, or buy anything sold or processed, or process anything sold, bought, or processed, or repair anything sold, bought, or processed. You know, as a career, I don't want to do that." See *http://www.imdb.com/title/tt0098258/quotes.*

5 See Neil Postman, *The End of Education: Redefining the Value of School* (Vintage, 1994) and Ken Robinson, *Out of Our Minds: Learning to Be Creative* (Capstone, 2001).

The dangerous life of ideas

Quick test: Name five new ways to change the world, or you will die!

Sorry, time's up. Fortunately, I can't kill anyone from this side of the book, and writers killing readers is bad business. But if I did honor the threat, you'd be dead. No one can come up with one big idea, much less five, that fast. As absurd as this paragraph is so far, it mirrors how adults often manage creative thinking: "be creative, and perfect, right now." Whenever ideas are needed because of a crisis or a change, there's a fire-drill call, an immediate demand. But rarely is the call met with sufficient resources— namely time—to mine those ideas. The bigger the challenge, the more time it will take to find ideas, but few remember this when criticizing ideas to death moments after they've been born.

Cynical idea-killing phrases like, "that never works," "we don't do that here," or "we tried that already" are common (see "The list of negative things innovators hear" in Chapter 4) and can easily make idea finding environments more like slaughterhouses than gardens. It's as if an idea knocks on the door, and someone answers waving an Uzi: "Go away! I'm looking for ideas." Ideas need nurturing and are grown, not manufactured, which suggests that idea shortages are self-inflicted. It doesn't take a genius to recognize that ideas will always be easier to find if they're not shot down on sight.

The myth that leads to this idea-destroying behavior is that good ideas will look the part when found. When Henry Ford made his first automobiles—awkward, smelly machines that stalled, broke down, and failed even the most generous comparisons to horses— people judged the superficial aspects, not the potential (see Figure 6-1). Everyone believes the future will come all at once in a neatly gift-wrapped package, as if Horse 2.0, whatever its incarnation, would make its first appearance with trumpets blaring and angels hovering above. The future never enters the present as a finished product, but that doesn't stop people from expecting it to arrive that way.

The idea of the computer mouse (see Figure 6-2) was equivalently weird and uninspiring to pre-PC age eyes ("Wow, a block of wood on a cord! The future is here!"). Evaluating new ideas flat

Figure 6-1. Would you see this idea, a flimsy gas-powered cart called the quadcycle, as the future of transportation in 1898? Most people then didn't either. This is one of Henry Ford's first automobiles.

out against the status quo is pointless. New ideas demand new perspectives, and it takes time to understand, much less judge, a point of view. Flip a world map or this book upside down, and at first it will feel bizarre. But wait. Observe for a few moments, and soon the new perspective will become comprehendible and possibly useful. However, that bizarre initial feeling tells you nothing about the value of the idea—it's an artifact of newness, not goodness or badness. This means using statements like "this hasn't been done before" or "that's too weird" alone to kill ideas is creative suicide: no new idea can pass that bar (see the upcoming sidebar "Idea killers").

How to find good ideas

To open minds and find good ideas, return to the kid in the park. What is it about his attitude that allows fearless idea exploration? Linus Pauling, the only winner of two solo Nobel Prize awards in history, had this to say about finding ideas: "The best way to have

Figure 6-2. The superficials of innovation are rarely impressive. This is a version of the first computer mouse.

a good idea is to have lots of ideas." This sounds idiotic to most ears because it cuts against the systematic, formulaic, efficiency-centric perspective worshiped in schools and professions. It seems wasteful to follow Pauling's advice. Can't we just skip to the good ideas? Optimize the process? Memorize a formula to plug stuff into? Well, you can't.

The dirty little secret—the fact often denied—is that unlike the mythical epiphany, real creation is sloppy. Discovery is messy; exploration is dangerous. No one knows what he's going to get when he's being creative. Filmmakers, painters, inventors, and entrepreneurs describe their work as a search: they explore the unknown hoping to find new things worth bringing to the world. And just like other kinds of explorers, the search for ideas demands risk: much of what's found won't be satisfactory. Therefore, creative work cannot fit neatly into plans, budgets, and schedules. Magellan, Lewis and Clark, and Captain Kirk were all sent on missions into the unknown with clear understanding that they might not return with anything, or even return at all.

The lives of well-known creative thinkers are filled with compulsions for playing with ideas: they wanted wide landscapes to explore. Beethoven obsessively documented every idea he had, madly scribbling them on tree trunks or on the manuscript paper he had jammed into his clothing, even interrupting meals and conversations to scratch them down.[6] Ted Hoff, the inventor of the first microprocessor (Intel 4004) used to tell his team that ideas were a dime a dozen, encouraging them not to obsess or fixate on any particular one until a wide range of ideas had been explored. Hemingway made dozens of rewrites and drafts, changing plots, characters, and themes before he published his novels. WD-40 is named because of the 40 attempts it took to get it right (Dr. Ehrlich's cure for syphilis, called Salvarsan 606, was similarly named). Picasso used eight notebooks to explore the ideas for just one of his paintings (*Guernica*); if you watch the film *The Mystery of Picasso*, you can watch the master exploring ideas, good and bad, in real time as he creates dozens of paintings (see Figure 6-3).[7]

Figure 6-3. Many artists use canvases to explore ideas as they paint—they're not painting by numbers, but exploring and making mistakes as they create.

[6] Edmund Morris, *Beethoven: The Universal Composer* (HarperCollins, 2005).

[7] The film the *The Mystery of Picasso* (Dir. Henri-Georges Clouzot, Image Entertainment) is a classic of art schools everywhere. Few artists, much less legends, were as open to documenting their process as Picasso, as demonstrated by this film. Make sure to listen to the DVD commentaries, as they provide more insight than the spare soundtrack. See *http://www.imdb.com/title/tt0049531/*.

Idea killers

These are phrases for thoughtless idea rejection. They're used by people who are too lazy to give useful criticism or direction, who fail to ask idea-provoking response questions, or who dismiss others not believed to have the potential for good ideas. Phrases like "it's not in our budget" or "we don't have time" are half-truths, as budgets and schedules can be changed for a sufficiently good idea. Others are idiotic, such as "we've never done that before," which is a condition of any new idea, good or bad.

- We tried that already.
- We've never done that before.
- We don't do it that way here.
- That never works.
- Not in our budget.
- Not an interesting problem.
- We don't have time.
- Executives will never go for it.
- It's out of scope.
- People won't like it.
- It won't make enough money.
- How stupid are you?
- You're smarter with your mouth shut.

A complete list of idea killers is at *http://www.scottberkun.com/blog/?p=492.*

The list goes on. In any field, creatives are those who dedicate themselves to generating, working, and playing with ideas. Pattie Maes, director of MIT Media Lab's interactive group, explains:

> *Most of the work that we do is like this. We start with a half-baked idea, which most people—especially critical people—would just shoot down right away or find uninteresting. But when we start working on it and start building, the ideas evolve. That's really the method that we use at the Media Lab…in the process of building something we often discover the interesting problems and the interesting things…that leads to interesting discoveries.*

There is further support for an innovator's desire to seek out new ideas. In a recent survey, innovative people—from inventors to scientists, writers to programmers—were asked what techniques they used. Over 70% believed they got their best ideas by exploring areas they were not experts in (see Figure 6-4).[8] The ideas found during these explorations often sparked new ways to think about the work in their own domain. And since they didn't have as many preconceptions as the people in that field, they could find new uses for what were seen as old ideas. Doctors studied film production; writers read biographies of painters. Any pool of ideas, no matter how foreign, could become a new area of discovery for an open mind.

Figure 6-4. Based on a recent online survey of over 100 self-identified innovators in various fields.

Like the child in the park, creativity is intertwined with the ability to see ideas as fluid, free things. Ideas come, they go, and that's OK; to an open mind, ideas are everywhere (something I'll prove momentarily). It's the willingness to explore, experiment, and play, to invest energy, hit a dead end, and then chase a new direction that allows minds to find good ideas. All of our notions of play, and its freedoms from formal judgment, are inexplicably linked to finding good ideas.

---

[8] *http://www.scottberkun.com/blog/?p=422.*

Ideas and filters

For all my trumpeting of open-minded thinking, it's true that wandering the Library of Congress looking at random ideas won't result in the Nobel Prize. We're asked to find ideas to solve problems, and even if idea finding approximates explorative play, it has to eventually wander back into something resembling work.

The secret to balancing work and play is thinking of the mind as a filter. Instead of binary switches—open vs. closed, creative vs. routine—we want a sliding scale of openness that we can control. If you want new ideas, you have to slide toward openness, turning some filters off, exploring thoughts you'd ordinarily reject offhand. Do this until some interesting ideas are found; then, gradually turn more filters on until you're left with a handful that are both good and practical for the problem at hand. Choosing which filters to apply when has much to do with successful innovation; it's not just having an open mind, it's also knowing when to postpone certain judgments, and then when to bring them back in. If a mind is always open, it never finishes anything; if a mind is never open, it never starts.

We live most moments with many filters. Consider eyesight: at best we see 160 degrees around us, less than 50% of the visual information nearby. Dogs hear more sounds and cats smell more odors than we do. Even as children, we learn rules of conduct and behavior, filtering out possibilities both to be safe and to fit into society. And, perhaps worse for creativity, as adults we aim for efficiency in our time, shortcutting through days, looking for fast tracks and power tools. The trap of efficiency is that it's not how explorers or inventors do their jobs: they turn their filters off for long stretches of time, trying to go where others haven't been. They wander into inconvenience, and danger, purposefully. Even when tasked with being creative, most people most of the time apply filters too soon.

The history and misuse of brainstorming

The term *brainstorm* has been abused and bastardized in the 50 years since its coinage. The concept originates with Alex F. Osborn, whose excellent book *Applied Imagination* launched the industry of business creativity books.[9] Its rise to popularity led to the quick misuse of the technique as a panacea for every conceivable business problem. When it failed to do the impossible of tripling people's IQs, reversing executive stupidity, or instantly transforming dysfunctional teams, the business world turned against it, despite its fundamental goodness. Those who still use the term apply it trivially: when they find an interesting idea, they call it a brainstorm—"I had a brainstorm for reorganizing my stamp collection binder."

The true essence of brainstorming as a method is well described in *Applied Imagination*, a fantastic read and a forgotten classic. The core message is simple:

• You have three things: facts, ideas, and solutions.

• You need to spend quality time with all of them.

The great mistake is leaping from facts to solutions, skipping over the play and exploration at the heart of finding new ideas. Most of us are experienced with finding facts—they're beaten into us throughout schools and colleges, and modern media pummels us with more. We're also familiar with solutions, which are the end results that pay the bills and explain why we've survived in the world. But idea finding? What's that? It's what few adults are patient enough to do, yet it's at the heart of creativity (the child in the park) and brainstorming (as defined by Osborn).

• **Fact finding.** The work of collecting data, information, and piles of research about whatever it is that needs to be done.

• **Idea finding.** The exploration of possibilities—free from as many constraints as possible—and using or ignoring facts as needed to find more ideas.

• **Solution finding.** The development of promising ideas into solutions that can be applied to the world.

Finding ideas and turning off filters

Osborn researched which environments stimulated people's creativity, and this study led to the following four idea-finding (aka brainstorming) rules:

---

[9] Alex F. Osborn, *Applied Imagination* (Charles Scribner's Sons, 1957).

1. Produce as many ideas as possible

2. Produce ideas as wild as possible

3. Build upon each other's ideas

4. Avoid passing judgment

Rule #1 sets the goal on volume, not quality (think Beethoven, Hoff, and Pauling). Since we don't know which ideas have value until we've explored them, spliced them together, or played with their many combinations, we want a big landscape. According to Osborn, a group of four or five properly led people can continually find new ideas for anything for a half-hour to an hour, producing 50 or 100 ideas before running out of steam.

Rule #2 encourages the crossing of boundaries and the saying of illogical, unexpected, and unpredictable things. Without these rules, we naturally inhibit what we say for fear of embarrassment: if you set outrageousness as a goal and reward it, you help turn that filter off, opening up the chance to find truly original ideas. Sometimes asking for the worst ideas for a particular problem can take you in entertaining directions, leading to places you'd never otherwise go. Have you ever been lost in a bad neighborhood in a new city, only to find a fantastic shop or restaurant? Discovery can have any origin, and Rule #2 forces exploration. If nothing controversial, weird, or embarrassing is said in a brainstorming session, you've violated Rule #2.

Rule #3, like Dan Bricklin's combination of innovations to invent VisiCalc, encourages the combination of ideas to forces creative thinking through hybrids and idea breeding. No ideas are 100% new: they're all combinations of something and something. Making this explicit prevents people from suppressing ideas for fear of stepping on, or changing, an idea mentioned by someone else. NIH (not invented here) syndrome, where ideas from others are rejected, is a clear violation of Rule #3.

Finally, Rule #4 takes us back to the secret of the kid in the park. Judgment isn't necessary during exploration—we don't know enough about the possibilities, so why would we reject or accept any idea? Would you buy the first car you sat in? Marry the first woman you met? When finding ideas, everyone needs to know his ideas won't be judged until later. And if the goal is volume (Rule

#1), there's no need to evaluate the initial thought, only to write it down so it can be explored later. Judgment is all too easy, and there's no harm in holding it back awhile to give those ideas a fighting chance.

However, there are limitations. When done in groups, the human dynamics of social situations come into play. Is everyone trying to kiss up to the boss? Does Fred always hog the floor? Is Jack afraid to say anything? Designating a skilled facilitator keeps things flowing and fair, and ensures that the rules are followed and that the meeting runs only as long as needed. The vibe should approximate the playful environment of a park: a fun, low-stress, free time to try things out, awaken dormant imaginations, and take pleasure in chasing new ideas.

Proof that ideas are everywhere

One game, famous in improvisation, is called "What Is This?" Look at any object around you: a pen, a cup, this book. Ask yourself, what else can it be used for? Take, for starters, this book in your hand: it's a doorstop, a weapon, a plate, a way to get your boss to be less of an idiot, a waste of $25, and on it goes. Play this game with a friend and see who can come up with more.

The point is that anything can be used for things other than its intended purpose. We assume everything has one function, but that's wrong: you can use anything for anything (although it might not work well, you can try). There's nothing stopping you from using this book as underwear or to paper your walls. The game forces you to turn your filters off.

Many great ideas come from the repurposing of one thing for something else. Laser beams were used to make CD players and supermarket checkout scanners. Even attempting to reuse something in a novel way, and failing, can lead to ideas no one else has thought of before. Play the game with items you use in your work or with failed projects just asking for reuse, and you'll soon find yourself off and running with an abundance of good ideas.

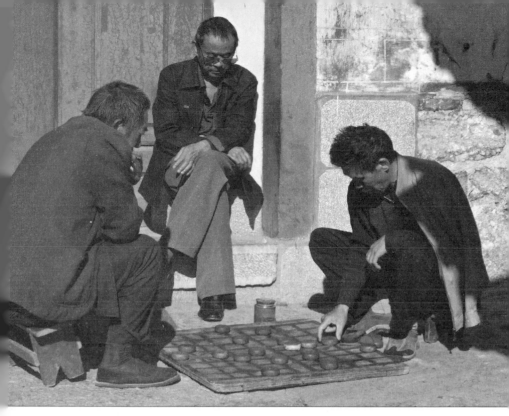

CHAPTER 7

Your boss knows more about innovation than you

What advice would typical executives give Stephen Hawking, one of the brightest living minds, if he worked for them? Would they ask him to write daily status reports? Defend his action items from PowerPoint slides at team debrief meetings? Of similar curiosity is whether Steve Wozniak, Albert Einstein, or Isaac Newton ever filled out time cards, wrote performance reviews, or had their ideas ranked on scorecards by committees of middle managers. Could you imagine Mozart, da Vinci, or Marie Curie sitting next to each other, taking notes, at an all day company-wide event? It's hard to see any of these commonplace situations working out well for the prospect of innovation.

If we struggle to imagine past innovators doing amazing things in our workplaces, what makes us think we can do creative work in them? Talent is only as good as the environment it's in. If we threw Shakespeare or Bach into a creative dungeon, lashing them when ideas entered their minds, odds are against them being creative for long, if at all.

Few managers recognize that their training and experience, designed to protect what exists, work against the forces needed for innovation. The history of management—lurking beneath the hot trends of *Harvard Business Review* and *Fast Company* magazine—is rooted in factories, banks, and railroads, not in invention, creative thinking, or revolution. And while it's easy to see the impossibility of managing creative teams with the techniques of assembly lines, many managers do, trapping good ideas in systems structured to work against them.

The myth that managers know what to do

Here's an experiment: close this book, look at the back cover, and turn it upside down. Really, do it. Please? Pretty please with sugar on top? Look, I'm the author of this book and I'm giving you a direct order. Do it now or I'll stop writing. I'll wait. (Imagine me at my desk, twiddling my writerly thumbs, bored out of my mind, waiting for you to stop reading this sentence and become an obedient reader, flipping the book to examine the back cover. Look, it's worth it, I swear on this book.) OK, now that you're back, let's chat about what just happened, in the context of power and talent.

Even if reading this book has been the worst slog of your life, I bet you checked the back cover anyway. The reason is simple: as the author, I have power. You assume I know what I'm doing. But there is a difference between power and talent. You didn't look at the back cover because of how talented I am: you did it because I, being the all-powerful god-like voice of the page, told you to. (Now, send me six frosted cupcakes, a case of pale ale, and 12 million dollars in small, unmarked bills.[1])

Similar confusion reigns in the workplace. Those in power can make decisions others can't, but that doesn't mean they have the wisdom or experience to do it well. Every rock star innovator has worked for someone who couldn't innovate his way out of his pants. But we deny this because we often want to believe, despite evidence to the contrary, that those with authority are as talented as they are powerful. Faith in this idea makes working for them tolerable, as it offers an explanation, however false, for why *we* are working for *them*. There are exceptional managers out there, stars worthy of their power and more, but they're hard to find. The rest of the time innovators must beware of their own myth-making: it's easy to overlook peoples' lack of talent by misplacing faith in their power.

Why managers fail

This book has emphasized the point that no one knows what's possible. Every great innovation had dozens of leading minds laughing it out the door. Chester Carlson, the inventor of the first copy machine, was told the technology he needed would never exist. Lord Calvin, one of the great physicists of the 19th century, said machines heavier than air could never fly. Right now, powerful managers, even the cute ones who appear on magazine covers, are failing to predict the future. There is no innovation oracle. Futurists, like Buckminster Fuller or Nicholas Negroponte (founder of MIT's Media Lab), make their livings being wrong

---

[1] The psychology of authority is not a joke. The seminal Milgram experiments proved just how willing we are to torture each other simply because we are told to do so. See *http://www.holah.karoo.net/milgramstudy.htm*.

most of the time.[2] It's beyond human comprehension to know with any certainty what will happen next.

Yet somehow when people bring a new idea to their manager, they forget the fallibility of prediction. It's easy to assume that the manager has a better perspective on the viability of an idea, perhaps from her superior experience and knowledge of the industry. But these are exactly the factors that also work against innovation: high experience and confidence make people the greatest resistors to new ideas as they have the most to lose (see "The innovator's dilemma explained" in Chapter 4). The managers of propeller aircraft design were the last to adopt jet engines. Same for graphic user interfaces vs. command lines, telephones vs. telegraphs, and—as hard as it is to admit—for whatever we're using now vs. whatever is coming next.

It's natural for people to protect what they know instead of leaping into the unknown, and managers are no exception. Managers might even be worse, as the politics they rely on to survive can make them more entrenched and defensive. Drucker wrote, "management tends to believe that anything that has lasted for a fair amount of time must be normal and go on forever. Anything that contradicts what we have come to consider a law of nature is then rejected as unsound." And since few managers are aware of these natural biases, or trained to overcome them, they're unprepared for the day the future—in the guise of a half-baked, curiously shaped idea—knocks on their door. It's not a question of intelligence or intention—it's a willingness to re-evaluate management's purpose.

The conflicts of management and innovators

Professional management was born from the desire to optimize and control, not to lead waves of change. Frederick Taylor, Henry Ford, Henry Laurence Gantt (of charting fame), the fathers of professional management, believed it should be a reductive science. The goal was to minimize chance, optimize performance, and take control away from individuals. Decades before the first MBA

---

2 Buckminster Fuller coined the word *synergy*, among many other creations. It's a nice reminder that all words were invented by someone, and it's silly to bemoan the addition of new words to languages.

graduates dreamed of well-paying consulting jobs, Mr. Taylor, the father of management, studied the inefficiencies in factory workers; stopwatch in hand, he took notes, did time studies, and prescribed methods for faster performance. That's right: the making of widgets, hinges, nuts, and bolts is what drove the creation of business management.[3] Called scientific or classical management, the philosophy centers on designing jobs with repetitive tasks, and rewards the manager for optimizing their performance in measurable terms—for example, widgets made per minute (see Figure 7-1).

Figure 7-1. The management philosophy for running assembly lines can never create an innovation like the assembly line. Ford's first moving car assembly line, 1913.

If this seems like ancient history, remember that the automobile, oil, and railroad industries of the 19th and early 20th centuries fueled the economic growth of the United States. The success of these industries both legitimized Taylor and created wealth used to start or fund many well-known business schools of today

---

3 To go back before Taylor, you can find other management theorists. The military has the oldest management traditions because they were the first with the need to organize large groups of people for controlled tasks.

(Vanderbilt, Stanford, Harvard, MIT Sloan, and others).[4] Despite how progressive some modern management programs are, their roots are in a tradition most unkind to innovation. Management as a discipline is steeped in an old-school command and control attitude that is alive and well in the Internet Age.

To be fair, most management, most of the time, is sensibly directed at maintaining good business. It's hard enough to keep a business profitable and a team of people working together effectively; if an organization is healthy and successful, it makes sense for its leaders to act in ways that conserve those good things (although Talyorism isn't the way).[5] However, when managers raise the flag of innovation, the goals change, and the methods must follow. Many depend solely on Taylor-inspired behavior as a rule, regardless of what the goals demand. These folks are easy to spot: they might know buzzwords or talk of seeking breakthroughs, but they avoid all risks, never yield creative authority, and operate with self-centric hierarchical control over the flow of ideas. Like an assembly line, these managers hold tight to the notion that they are the sole possessors of intelligence, and must exercise regular control over workers capable only of the menial tasks of production.

Amy C. Edmonson, professor of management at Harvard Business School, agrees, "Management 101 is...based on the assumption that we know with a high degree of certainty what needs to happen...that is simply an outmoded concept, but we still use the same management tools: a production mindset."[6] To lead innovation requires rethinking who a manager is, what success feels like, and which tactics work. And to do that, we have to look back at managers of past innovations.

---

[4] Vanderbilt and Stanford, founders of eponymous universities, were railroad tycoons. Harvard Business School's first campus was funded by George Fisher Baker, president of the First National Bank. The MIT Sloan school is named after Alfred P. Sloan, chairman of the board of General Motors.

[5] Taylor was right about one thing: at the time, production was inefficient, and he deserved praise for asking new questions. However, he failed to empower workers by involving them in improving efficiency. Many workers have ideas for improvements and will suggest them if rewarded—a strategy Taylor never considered and which may have been more efficient than his own (were all those studies necessary? I can imagine workers laughing behind Taylor's back as he took weeks to discover inefficiencies they noticed their first day).

[6] Kelley Holland, *Under New Management, http://www.nytimes.com/2006/11/05/business/yourmoney/05mgmt.html*

Five challenges of managing innovation

I've reviewed the histories of hundreds of innovative projects from different industries, team sizes, and eras, and distilled five traits that managers of those efforts applied. Of course, this is not a guarantee: exceptions can be found of leaders following these and failing, as well as those who ignored them but still had success (see Chapter 3). However, the patterns are strong enough to apply widely, including start-up companies, solo efforts, ad-hoc groups, or even innovative projects in large organizations. No matter how many people are involved, these five challenges are faced by someone and must be overcome to bring the innovation to the world:

1. Life of ideas
2. Environment
3. Protection
4. Execution
5. Persuasion

The life of ideas

Ideas are everywhere. Chapter 6 explored some of the basics of creative thinking, but the life of ideas is bigger than what happens in brainstorming meetings. The best idea-finding sessions in the world are useless if that creative energy doesn't go anywhere. Ideas don't do much—it's what's done with them that matters. Are they funded? Encouraged? Used to reinvent and rethink? Given time to grow? Rewarded with cash prizes or trips to Hawaii? Are people pushed to explore, prototype, follow their instincts, and learn from what happens?

Teams with healthy idea life cycles are easy to spot: ideas flow between people easily and in large volumes. Conversations are vibrant with questions and suggestions, prototypes and demos happen regularly, and people commit to finding and fighting for good ideas. Often, this is fun; people are happy to learn from failures, debates, and bizarre ideas. Teams that innovate are great places for ideas to live—like happy pets, they're treated well, get lots of attention, and are shared among people who care deeply about them.

The life of ideas is the responsibility of whoever is in charge. He defines it by his responses and behavior, especially when he's challenged by someone else's ideas. For example, if someone asks, "Hey boss, can we have status meetings over lunch to save time?" and the boss replies, "Say something that stupid again and you're fired," no one will ask similar questions. All ideas about improving the status meeting, and perhaps improving anything, are dead forevermore. Or, more typically, if no ideas from anyone other than the manager are ever chosen, people will eventually stop proposing suggestions.

Teams with scorched deserts where creative jungles should be usually have a manager to blame. The boss must attend to the life of ideas for all the people he works with, investing time and money to nurture their young ideas, granting room for them to breathe, and supporting the ideas' development, delivery, and recycling (to make way for new ones).

The environment

Alan Kay, a member of the legendary group at Xerox PARC, said this about his manager, Bob Taylor: "His attitude kept it safe for others to put aside fears and ego and concentrate objectively on the problem at hand."[7] According to many accounts, Taylor encouraged a free discourse of ideas, including open criticism and debate, in a weekly meeting in a room filled with beanbag chairs. The goal wasn't to roast each other, but to push, prod, cajole, share, inspire, and enrage as needed to give life to everyone's best ideas.[8] The environment put innovation at the center, with politics, posturing, and hierarchy on the perimeter. This can go as far as office architecture because people's ability to feel creative and share ideas is heavily influenced by how their offices, shared spaces, and buildings are designed.

---

[7] Douglas K. Smith and Robert C. Alexander, *Fumbling the Future: How Xerox Invented, Then Ignored, the Personal Computer* (iUniverse, 1999), 79.

[8] An excellent exploration of the manager's role in creative environments can be found in Jerry Hirshberg, *The Creative Priority: Driving Innovative Business in the Real World* (Collins, 1999). The book is based on his experience as director of Nissan design and explains the role of tension in creative environments (he calls it *creative abrasion*).

Tom Kelly, general manager of IDEO and author of *The Art of Innovation*,[9] explains:

> *Innovation flourishes in greenhouses. What do I mean by a greenhouse? A place where the elements are just right to foster the growth of good ideas. Where there's heat, light, moisture, and plenty of nurturing. The greenhouse we're talking about, of course, is the workplace, the way spaces take shape in offices and teams work together.*

Lewis Thomas, author of *Lives of a Cell*[10] and former dean of the Yale Medical School, wrote:

> *One way to tell when something important is going on is by laughter. It seems to me that whenever I have been around a laboratory at a time when something very interesting has happened, it has at first seemed to be quite funny. There's laughter connected with the surprise—it does look funny. And whenever you hear laughter...you can tell that things are going well and that something probably worth looking at has begun to happen in the lab.*

That laughter, in part, means people are comfortable with and unafraid of new ideas. The Nerf toys, open architecture, and fun vibe at Google's headquarters (see Chapter 1) aren't gimmicks; the environment is supportive of ideas and collaboration, which helps innovations move through the organization.

Hiring and team structure may define the working environment more than other factors combined. Taylor hired with innovation in mind, recruiting people who naturally challenged the status quo and were self-driven pursuers of their imaginations. He wanted people who thrived on the uncertainties of doing new things, who could drive ideas forward. Taylor viewed his management role not as a grand creator or assembly-line foreman, but as an enabler of other people's ideas. And it worked—his team developed the laser printer, Ethernet, object-oriented computing, and the graphical user interface (GUI). Good managers of innovation recognize that they are in primary control over the environment, and it's up to them to create a place for talented people to do their best work.

---

[9] Tom Kelley et al., *The Art of Innovation* (Currency/Doubleday, 2001).

[10] Lewis Thomas, *Lives of a Cell: Notes of a Biology Watcher* (Penguin, 1978).

The protection

One thing a genius can't do that his manger can is provide cover fire. Whether through power, inspiration, or charisma, managers have the singular burden of protecting their teams. Innovations always threaten someone in power, and executives in search of budget cuts frequently target them first. The manager's unique role is to use whatever means necessary to shield innovation while it's too young to defend itself in the open. Steve Jobs took the Macintosh project into a separate building at Apple headquarters, sequestering it from the rest of the company. The first laptop at Toshiba was rejected by corporate leaders, and Tetsuya Mizoguchi, the team leader, fought to keep the project alive until he won executive support; three years later, the product had 38% of the market.[11] Any story of breakthrough work has someone acting as a shield, defending innovation while it's happening.

One of Thomas Edison's secret weapons was his star persona. His ego may have been large, but he used his stardom as a shield for his research lab: his true engine of innovation. His team of bright minds—a dozen inventors in Menlo Park, New Jersey—worked happily in relative anonymity, free from public scrutiny or the stresses of appearances and interviews. Many major insights of developing the electric light and the phonograph are attributed to his staff, not to Edison himself. Edison took the heat for ideas that failed, and by making himself an easy target for investors and the public, he protected his team from all kinds of negative influences.[12]

All innovations run on political capital: the lifeline of budget and staff comes from somewhere, and everyone (including the project leader) is in competition for those limited resources. Even famed start-up companies that began in garages had to be defended from frustrated spouses or sarcastic teenagers who wanted those resources for more traditional purposes (families are as political as any organization). Life is a zero-sum game, and the resources for innovation must come at the expense of something else.

---

[11] From *Diffusion of Innovations*, 145.

[12] Andrew Hargadon, *How Breakthroughs Happen: The Surprising Truth About How Companies Innovate* (Harvard Business School Press, 2003).

Successful innovators compare their ambitions to their capital. If a project needs more time, money, or political cover fire than its leader can provide, the effort will be discovered, lobotomized, or killed. For example, if the manager bets on promises for budget (or loans) that are withdrawn, or makes claims that he fails to deliver, the effort will die of starvation no matter how many great ideas, creative environments, or amazing talents it has. And if he's too conservative and doesn't take enough risks, the project might survive, but it will not be progressive enough to achieve its goals. It's a tightrope to walk—pushing a project hard enough without pushing it too far—but every successful innovator has done the same balancing act since the beginning of time.

Protecting innovation includes obtaining funding, finding allies, protecting teams from natural predators (defenders of status quo, jealous managers, the ever-resilient and contagious threat of organizational idiocy), and even buffering the team and its stars from their self-destructive tendencies. Sometimes protecting an innovative team will demand withholding information that might discourage the team (for example, a VP's napalm-laced feedback), testing the manager's judgment, boundaries, and willingness to make psychological sacrifices for the project. Managers can take larger bullets for the team than anyone else.

The execution

Ideas are abstractions. You can't get cash from the idea of an ATM machine, nor commute home on the notion of a hovercraft. To become an innovation, an idea has to blossom into whatever form necessary—a demo, a prototype, a product—to be useful to people. To shepherd an idea down the long, arduous path from conception to realization is known as *execution*. And despite its workman-like reputation in comparison to creative thought, executing on an idea is the hardest task faced by managers of innovation. In Chapter 6, we explored how easy ideas are to find; the challenge is doing all the work necessary to manifest them in the world. We know the names Edison, Wright, Wozniak, and Tesla not because they had grand ideas alone, but because they were able to execute on them before their competitors. Steve Jobs was right when he said, "Real artists ship," to rally the Macintosh team into putting in the long, exhausting, unglamorous hours needed to get the product out the door.[13]

Execution forces managers to deal with the countless details that were waved away during brainstorms and demos. All the challenges swept under the rug of "we'll deal with it later" or "that's not important now" become immovable roadblocks, demanding attention now; otherwise, progress stops. These sacrifices are often difficult for idealists to handle. Even though their passion is what convinced others to support their ideas, that passion must be tempered by compromises if those ideas are to make it to the world.

The challenge is making the right sacrifices at the right time in the right way: there is no formula for this, only the manager's and his team's judgment. Managers must balance the team on the edge of the ideals that drove the effort through early stages ("we will change the world!") and the necessary constraints of schedules and budgets to finish ("we must ship in four weeks, do or die"). Too much idealism, and the work never ships—not enough, and little change is brought to the world.

Persuasion

Innovation champions—like Jeff Hawkins (Palm), Steve Jobs (Apple), and Bob Taylor (Xerox PARC)—have often needed to put down their swords and egos to pitch their projects for all they're worth. Innovators never have all the cards, so they must ask others for help to make things happen: start-ups have investors; films have production companies; businesses take loans from banks. Earlier, we explored why people don't like new ideas, and the questions people with new ideas face. Well, this is true for managers, but the stakes are higher: they're not only responsible for their ideas, but also for the collective hopes of an entire team.

All innovation heroes survived the closing of doors in their faces: Carlson (Xerox), Jobs (Apple II), Page and Brin (Google), and Smith (FedEx). As persuasive as these greats might have been, they weren't convincing enough to prevent rejections. We imagine great

---

13 *http://www.folklore.org/StoryView.py?project=Macintosh&story=Real_Artists_ Ship.txt.*

persuaders as charismatic figures, dazzling and romancing the soon-to-be-convinced with special powers, but real innovators are not magicians. The difference between success and failure is most often relentlessness, not talent or charisma (though those help). Jobs explains, "I'm convinced that about half of what separates the successful entrepreneurs from the non-successful ones is pure perseverance."[14] Persuasion is a skill; if sufficiently motivated, anyone can improve.[15]

Persuasion is needed to start a project, recruit top people, obtain resources, convince talent (or spouses) not to leave, as well as to compel investors or customers to buy once there is something to sell. Persuasion fuels innovation at all levels, and every successful innovation depends on getting people to believe in things that have not been done before.

---

[14] *http://americanhistory.si.edu/collections/comphist/sj1.html.*
[15] Robert Cialdini, *Influence: Science and Practice* (Allyn & Bacon, 2000).

CHAPTER 8

The best ideas win

The best ideas don't always win, but that doesn't stop people from believing they should. Most innovators were frustrated by how their ideas, clearly superior in their own minds, struggled for acceptance in the world. Pick from any field at any time and you'll discover tales of dismay, depression, and anger fueled by the innovators' faith that their better ideas not only should, but will win out over others. Of course, visionary innovators are rarely objective in these matters, as often these so-called best ideas are conveniently their own.[1] Ted Nelson, the man who coined the phrase *hypertext*, laments the limitations of the World Wide Web, and he continues to fight for big ideas that predate the web browsers by decades. Douglas Engelbart and Alan Kay, pioneers of the personal computer, have similar exasperations about the grand ideas they pioneered from the 1970s that have yet to be realized.[2] Even social and political innovators like Martin Luther King, Gandhi, and Thomas Jefferson voiced similar righteousness about their ideas and the faith that the best ones should prevail.

It's not news that innovators are often idealists, but the myth that the best ideas win should not be underestimated. Notice how few people run around arguing that the worst idea wins or that their own inventions are rubbish. People have beliefs about what the world is or should be, and why some ideas, inventions, or people win out over others. Even the notions of best, good, win, and lose are opinions, as is the obsession with framing things in binary terms. Good vs. bad, best vs. worst, happy vs. sad are all tenuous constructions, as the world never divides into two easy piles (e.g., happy vs. sad neglects the existence of the bittersweet). However, that doesn't stop people from trying.

---

1 I've yet to find a solid reference for the relationship between egos, innovation, and achievement. One general reference is *Greatness: Who Makes History and Why*, by Dean Keith Simonton (The Guilford Press, 1994). However, as an anecdote, the wide majority of biographies I've read of great innovators includes great egos.

2 Doug Engelbart has done many interviews about his perception on his place in history, as well as the state of computing today. One example that briefly mentions his opinion of the current state of computing can be found in this short essay: *http://www.byte.com/art/9509/sec15/art1.htm*. Alan Kay has also offered many commentaries on the state on technology relative to better ideas being ignored; some of these ideas are touched on in this interview: *http://www.educause.edu/ir/library/html/erm/erm99/erm99027.html*.

It's clear at this point in the book that innovation is complex, has many meanings and factors, and can't be captured in the pithy quotes that make for good myths. As this chapter explains, there are many contributing factors, and it's impossible to remember them all, all the time. This is why the myth that the best idea wins is so dangerous. It plays possum, rolling on its back, looking cute and innocent, while it quietly reaches behind our backs, taps on our far shoulders with its furry little paw, and laughs as we turn away from the truth.

Why people believe the best wins

Fairy tales and hero stories follow similar patterns: good guys win, bad guys lose, and people who do the right thing get nice prizes.[3] These rules are pleasant, easy to remember, and have been with us as long as we've had stories to tell. In some cultures, including America, these stories of "goodness wins" extend to intellectual goodness and the making of good things. Americans hold ingenuity to be one of the best kinds of goodness, spotlighting it and projecting it into our local history: Benjamin Franklin's political inventiveness; the innovative tactics of Minutemen in the Revolutionary War (which weren't that innovative); and the industrial genius of Whitney, Fulton, Edison, Ford, Carnegie, and Steve Jobs. By the simplest definition, heroes are the best at what they do. America created Superman, not *Second-place*-man or *Sometimes-better-than-average*-guy.

Meritocracy—the ideal that the best do or should win—is a deeply held belief among Americans, and in part comprises the American Dream. Combined with the hero model (good guys win), there's a natural tendency to nudge the telling of history toward stories that fit both ideals and to whitewash, or ignore, those that don't. Whenever we don't know the full story of why someone or something won, the default assumptions are:

1. The victory was deserved: "Edison made the first lightbulb."

2. The victory was heroic: "Gutenberg paved the way for the Internet."

---

3 Of course, mythologies and fairy tales are numerous, and there are many patterns equally as prominent in various pantheons as wish fulfillment and hero quests. See *The Uses of Enchantment*, by Bruno Bettelheim (Penguin, 1991), or *The Hero with a Thousand Faces*, by Joseph Campbell (Princeton University Press, 1972).

Certainly most know that the best doesn't always win, but we don't go out of our way to uncover counterexamples either (much like the discussion in the section "Evolution and innovation" from Chapter 2). We accept stories that fit the patterns we know, as they provide happy feelings and encourage hope for how life *should be*. Victors of the past who won with dubious ethics or for questionable reasons—like Rockefeller, Carnegie, and Achilles—are remembered not for their flaws or unpopularity in their own time, but as heroes of achievement. Their victories and benevolent contributions, truths that fit the mythology, are the most popular stories we tell about their lives.[4] And should bad decisions be made, given enough time, the reasons for those judgments often fade, leaving only traditions of respect. Consider that the Liberty Bell, which cracked in half when first struck in 1753 and again decades later—clearly not well made or heroic in any way—is now a worshiped artifact of American history.[5] Or that Alfred Nobel, best known for founding the Nobel Peace Prize, made his fortune by inventing dynamite.[6]

The American pantheon of fictional legends includes MacGyver, James Bond, Indiana Jones, John McClane (from the film *Die Hard*), and Captain Kirk, invincible heroes who defeat evil at overwhelming odds by using good ideas, guile, and a healthy serving of gratuitous violence. They have better ideas, so they win. We're fond of creative idealism even at extremes, such as in stories like Ayn Rand's *The Fountainhead*, in which Howard Roark, a heroic architect, places his ideas above everything. Despite the complexity of the tale, the protagonist willingly sacrifices for his ideas. The simpler message often taken from this epic novel is that

---

4   The robber barrons are easy targets. Despite their label, today we experience only their philanthropic works, universities, and foundations. Carnegie had several incidents regarding workers rights, including the Homestead Strike of 1892 in which Frick, a manager under Carnegie, led the lockout of employees with arms, resulting in a riot and a dozen deaths. The icing on the ironic cake is that the park next to Carnegie-Mellon University in Pittsburgh is named Frick Park, and most students know his name for this benevolent reason alone. See *http://www.pbs.org/wgbh/amex/carnegie/peopleevents/pande04.html*.

5   The Liberty Bell didn't get its name until 1835. It has quite a story of misfortunes, some of which are likely myths themselves. See *http://www.libertybellmuseum.com/faqs.htm*.

6   Nobel was enigmatic, and not much is certain about his view of his own work. However, the creation of the Nobel prizes happened at his death as specified in his will. See *http://www.britannica.com/nobel/micro/427_33.html*.

good should win over bad, and if a better idea is ignored, the world is to blame ("the hostility of second-hand souls"). This belief goes further than meritocracy; the world's sense of what is best is less important than the individual's.

Applied to business, the myth that goodness wins is best captured in the famous saying, "If you build a better mousetrap, the world will beat a path to your door." It's sometimes paraphrased as "If you build it, they will come," the iconic phrase from the baseball film *Field of Dreams*. Unfortunately, the quote is a misattribution to Ralph Waldo Emerson, a leading 19th-century intellectual. What he actually said was probably, "If a man has good corn, or wood, or boards, or pigs to sell, you will find a broad, hard-beaten road to his house."[7] I'm not sure when you last sold pigs or grew corn, but Emerson had something other in mind than rallying would-be entrepreneurs to get in the innovation game. The phrase was meant to be poetic, not instructional, and he'd be disappointed at how many people have taken his words literally.

The phrase has been used as the entrepreneur's motto, misguiding millions into entertaining the notion that a sufficiently good idea will sell itself. As nice as it would be for good ideas to take responsibility for themselves, perhaps using their goodness ID cards to cut ahead of stupid ideas in the popularity line, it's not going to happen. Even the (false) proverbial mousetrap, as historian John H. Lienhard notes, has about 400 patents for new designs filed annually in the U.S., and we can be certain that no one is beating down their doors.[8] More than 4000 mousetrap patents exist, yet only around 20 ever became profitable products. These days, the best equivalent to the metaphoric mousetrap is "to build a better web site," proven by the 30,000 software patents and 1 million web sites created annually.[9] Certainly not all of these efforts are motivated by wealth or wishful thinking, but many inventors still hope that the "If you build it, they will come" sentiment is alive and strong.

---

[7] Jack Hope, *A Better Mousetrap, American Heritage,* October 1996, Vol. 47, issue 6 (online at *http://www.americanheritage.com/articles/magazine/ah/1996/6/1996_6_90.shtml*).

[8] Ibid.

[9] *http://www.realgeek.com/230/us-software-patents-hit-record-high/.*

Lienhard, based on his study of innovations throughout history, challenges that faith:

> *Rarely if ever are the networks that surround an innovation in its earliest stages given the credit they are due...a better mousetrap, like anything else, will succeed only when those who envision the idea convince others to join in their new venture—as investors, suppliers, employees, retailers, customers, and even competitors.*

The goodness or newness of an idea is only part of the system that determines which ideas win or lose. When we bemoan our favorite restaurant going out of business ("but they make the best cannelloni!") or why our favorite band can't sell albums ("they have the best lyrics!"), we're focusing on the small part of the picture that effects us personally, which is only one factor in the environment determining its fate. These environmental, or secondary, factors have as much influence as the quality of the idea, the talent, or the innovation itself.

The secondary factors of innovation

The history of innovation reveals many ideas that dominate a field yet are derided by insiders. Any hi-tech device today follows the QWERTY keyboard model, a system not designed for efficiency or ergonomics. The Phillips screw is inferior to the lesser-known Robertson screw, a clever gem of industrial design.[10] The M-16, the most widely produced rifle in the world, has serious jamming and ease-of-use problems.[11] Fireplaces, staples in American cabins and homes, are one of the least efficient heating systems known to man. And HTML and JavaScript are far from the best software development languages, yet they're perhaps the most successful in history. The list goes on, despite the best wishes of all of the smart, goodness-motivated people throughout time. Even today,

---

[10] Witold Rybczynski, *One Good Turn: A Natural History of the Screwdriver and the Screw* (Scribner, 2001). See *http://inventors.about.com/od/sstartinventions/a/screwdriver.htm*.

[11] This is a disputed claim, and its accuracy depends on time. During the Vietnam War these complains were frequent, but some claims since the 1970s point to improved ammunition and other modifications that nullify these problems. I'm not an expert on this issue, but I did find enough evidence to confidently list it in this paragraph. Start with *http://www.manningaffordability.com/s&tweb/PUBS/M16Rifle/M16_Rifle.html*.

right now, ideas of all kinds that experts criticize—including those in your own fields of expertise—are gaining adoption.

In Chapter 4, the psychology of innovations' diffusion was explored, listing how individuals make choices that impact innovation adoption. Now, it's time for a broader analysis of influential factors. Looking at history, here are seven factors that play major roles:

- **Culture.** The Japanese invented firearms years before Europeans.[12] But their culture saw the sword as a symbol of their values: craftsmanship, honor, and respect. Despite the advantages of using firearms, the innovation was ignored and seen as a disgraceful way to kill (a sentiment echoed by the Jedi in *Star Wars* films). The best technology is only one view of innovation—how the innovation fits in a culture's values is often stronger. For example, imagine a device in the U.S. that gave you telepathy at work but required making lunch out of your neighbor's dog or being naked in public, two taboos of American culture. Innovations do change societies, but they must first gain acceptance by aligning with existing values.

- **Dominant design.** The QWERTY keyboard came along for the ride with the first typewriter. When Christopher Sholes created this layout, he didn't imagine millions of people using it—he just needed a design that wouldn't jam his mechanical keys. But once typewriters succeeded, the first computer designers wanted to ease people's transitions to their creations, so they copied the typewriter design. Many dominant designs achieve popularity on the back of another innovation. Better designs might follow, but to gain acceptance, they must improve on that dominant idea by a sufficient margin to justify the costs of the switch (e.g., re-learning how to type). The more dominant the design, the more expensive those costs are (e.g., try innovating, or unifying, the shape of electric plugs around the world).

- **Inheritance and tradition.** The U.S. rejection of the metric system is tied to tradition: America already knew the English system, so why learn another? (See "Space, metrics, and Thomas Jefferson," later in this chapter.) Some people confuse their

---

[12] From *The Evolution of Technology*, 189.

comfort for a belief with it actually being good; therefore, inherited ideas (including the evils of bigotry, ignorance, and urban legends) are often protected by the very people they hurt in the name of honoring the beliefs of their parents and the past. This is a specific cultural factor.

- **Politics: who benefits?** There's often little malice in political workings—people are simply acting in self-interest. In any situation, just ask: who benefits if we choose X, and who benefits if we choose Y? You can predict how people in power will respond to any new idea if you first calculate its impact on them. The interests of those in power influenced the adoption, or rejection, of every innovation in history. Hunger, war, and poverty are tough problems, but it's in someone's interest for those problems to continue. Any innovation aimed at solving those problems must consider politics for it to succeed.

- **Economics.** Innovation is expensive: will the costs of changing to the new thing be worth it? Everyone might agree that an innovation is better in the abstract, but the financing required might be impossible or the risks unreasonable. Dominant designs (see above) are expensive to replace. Often there is only time or money for innovating in one area; other innovations are rejected, not on their merits, but on their value to the priorities of the moment.

- **Goodness is subjective.** Get three people in a room and you'll get five definitions of goodness (see Chapter 10). Fireplaces, mentioned earlier, are popular because of how they look more so than how they function. Consumer differences in values, tastes, and opinions are rarely explored until after an innovation has been proposed, or even built, leaving innovators with creations the public does not want. Smart innovators study their customers, mastering their needs early enough that those factors can be useful. The often-used Beta vs. VHS example fits: a key factor in the success of VHS was tape length (three hours, enough for a feature film, to Beta's one hour), which was more important to consumers than Beta's superior video quality.[13]

---

13 *http://technology.guardian.co.uk/online/comment/story/0,12449,881780,00.html.*

- **Short-term vs. long-term thinking.** One part of goodness is time: how long does this innovation need to be used for? Many superior ideas are rejected by societies interested in cheaper, shorter-term gains. In the 1930s, major cities in the U.S. had public transportation—trolleys and tram systems modeled on successful designs from Europe. But in the rush of the 1950s, and the thrill of automotive power, those streetcars were removed and replaced with new lanes for cars. Today, many cities regret these changes and approximate trolleys with new light-rail systems. The goodness of ideas changes depending on how far into the future their impact is considered.

The next time you witness a great idea rejected, or a bad idea accepted, this list will help reveal the true factors at work. Up next is an examination of two innovations, revealing how these secondary factors have played out in the past.

Space, metrics, and Thomas Jefferson

On September 23, 1999, NASA's $300 million Mars *Orbiter*, flying through space millions of miles from Earth, fired its engines to slow it into orbit around Mars. Its 10-month journey complete, the craft flew silently above the Martian sky at a leisurely 12,000 miles per hour. It followed all its programmed instructions and was, as planned, turning behind Mars' dark side, disappearing for the first time. The command staff waited expectantly for the *Orbiter*, 10 years in the making, to reappear on the other side (see Figure 8-1). Ten minutes later, well past its expected timeline, it had not arrived. Mission control feared the worst. They searched the Mars atmosphere but there was nothing: the *Orbiter* was gone.

They'd learn later that the spacecraft entered the wrong orbit, flying too low. Instead of a routine trip around the planet, it approached at a deadly angle and was destroyed in the atmosphere. What took longer to understand was the cause. Somehow, somewhere, an equation failed to convert units from metric to English, and the $300 million *Orbiter* was sent on a path of certain destruction. It was doomed before it even launched.

Figure 8-1. *The poor little Mars Orbiter. Had Jefferson succeeded, the craft might have survived its trip to Mars.*

As is always the case, this failure had many causes. The *Orbiter* was part of the "Faster, Better, Cheaper" initiative at NASA to accelerate innovation by removing processes in the name of creative freedom, but it simultaneously increased risks—a common dilemma for managers of innovation (speed cuts both ways). But one link in the chain of failures is the metric system itself: why does the world, and particularly the U.S., still use two different systems of measurement?

The metric system has been in use for over 200 years. It's used by 190 of the 193 nations on this planet, and it has many advantages over the English system (explained shortly).[14] Cans of soda, like Coke or Pepsi, still list both English and Metric measurements (12 oz/354 ml) as an odd testament to a token compromise of policy—and a good idea ignored. Even the United Kingdom, the home of the English (foot/gallon/mile) system, moved on to metrics decades ago.

---

[14] As you'd expect, there is no end to the debate over the relative merits of English and metrics, as well as the costs of switching in the U.S. For details on international use of the metric system, see *http://lamar.colostate.edu/~hillger/*. For pro and con arguments, check out these sites: *http://www.metric4us.com/* and *http://ts.nist.gov/WeightsAndMeasures/Metric/mpo_home.cfm*.

The American story of metrics, a tale of proposed and denied innovation, begins with Thomas Jefferson. While serving as Secretary of State, he innocently proposed to the U.S. Government that they replace the English measurement system.[15] It's an odd mess of ad-hoc measurements from the Babylonian, Roman, and Saxon royalty, and it wasn't a system so much as a pile of half-baked traditions and blindly followed rules (see Inheritance and tradition in the previous list). The yard, for example, was defined by the length of the belts worn by kings (had they not been so rotund for their day, who knows what size our football fields would be). Endorsed by English monarchs through the ages, the system was adopted without question by the American colonies. But Jefferson was smart and a free thinker. He knew it wouldn't be hard to design a better system, and that it would be a great value to the new nation. He got to work and soon had a plan similar to what would be called metrics by France years later.

He divided the English foot into ten units called lines, and divided lines into ten units called points. Using tens, decimal math, made perfect sense to him as an easy way to convert between unit sizes. (Quick: how many ounces in a gallon? Cups in a quart? We have 10 fingers, and base-10 math makes many operations easy.) He made a similar decimalization of larger measures; adjusted the size of the foot, yard, and mile to fit scales of 10; and proposed this plan to Congress in 1789. Everything was great. He probably imagined decimalizing everything from units of time to expressions of love. The promise in young Jefferson's mind must have been high.

The proposal landed with a thud (approximately 4.5 kilograms of force per cubic centimeter). Congress didn't so much reject his plan as starve it to death: the idea was ignored (see Politics: who benefits?, Economics, and Short-term vs. long-term thinking in the previous list), and time went on. Across the Atlantic, the metric system was ratified in France in 1793 and spread over the decades into Europe's dominant system (although it was a slow, rocky process).[16] The opportunity for metrics to become dominant had much to do with the French Revolution, which ended just before

---

[15] Here's Jefferson simple proposal: *http://www.yale.edu/lawweb/avalon/jeffplan.htm*.
[16] *http://www.sciencemadesimple.com/metric_system.html#History*.

metrics were ratified. As a general lesson, large innovations, say, political revolution, bring with them many smaller changes for better or for worse. The metric system rode the wave of political innovation in France in a similar way to how the QWERTY keyboard rode the wave of technological innovation of the typewriter.

In 1866, the U.S. had no choice but to respond despite passing on the same idea 50 years earlier. Congress took action, but it was far from decisive. They drafted an act stating it was now legal—not required or encouraged, but legal—for people to use the metric system if they *chose*.[17] With promotion like that, how could the metric system lose? That's like a parent telling a child they're now allowed to clean their rooms thrice a day. Few Americans were moved, and the English measurements remained. There was little motivation for individual business owners to convert their equipment, no matter how much better Jefferson—or any objective thinker on the subject of measurement—thought of the matter. Several more anemic attempts were made to promote metrics, including the requirement for foods to be dual-labeled with metric and English measures (thus the soda cans), but to this day, no further effort has been made.

Some think situations like metrics in America need a forced hand: the only way a leap can be made is by mandate. For fun, imagine that you had evidence that replacing the QWERTY keyboard with a different design would create world peace or guarantee survival of the human race. What would have to be done to replace it around the world? In a single large country? In less than six months? Tasks like these are difficult because the costs of change are astronomical. Unless, like QWERTY's adoption, there is a larger wave of innovation that takes a replacement for QWERTY with it (or as is popular in sci-fi films, does away with keyboards entirely), it'd be hard to make any progress at all.

Some innovations—such as safety systems in automobiles or environmentally safe home construction (e.g., asbestos free)—succeeded only because governments provided incentives or penalties as motivation (in some cases, making the dominant design illegal). How else can progress happen in situations where the collective

---

17 *http://lamar.colostate.edu/~hillger/laws/metric-act.html.*

benefit for a society is greater than the perceived benefit for individuals? (For example, mandated elementary school is good for nations, but unpopular with children). However, some believe that forcing the hand of innovation goes against the nature of free markets and often backfires. The truth is complex; sometimes forcing innovation adoption works, and sometimes it doesn't. The best lesson in all cases is that success is defined more by the factors listed previously than by who is pushing the innovation—and how hard they're pushing it. Having $50 million to market a product means little compared to the forces of culture, dominant design, and politics.

To fully apply those factors to this example, the English system was the dominant design. While metrics had advantages, no one convinced the American politicians or people why the costs of making the changes were worth the effort. Thinking politically, what interests would be served by a businessman or a politician making the switch? And after Jefferson left office, why wasn't anyone willing to lead the charge for his proposal? The minority of those who benefited were set free after the 1866 act, but anyone on the fence never received incentive for change.

The goodness/adoption paradox

> The good is the enemy of the best.
>
> —Voltaire

Another excellent example of the tenuous relationship between an idea's goodness and its success is the technology behind the World Wide Web. When Tim Berners-Lee invented the Web, he didn't have the future of technological development in mind. His tool of choice for making web sites, called HTML, reflected simple notions for what documents would be like in the future. He didn't imagine the Web would have its own economy with bookstores and banks, nor was he thinking about the billions of personal and professional web sites that would become our primary way to communicate. Instead, he thought about scientific research papers, text-heavy one-way communication, because that's what the organization he worked for worried about.

His passion for simplicity was so great that he initially downplayed the role of images and media, focusing instead on text. For his purposes, HTML was lightweight, simple, and easy to learn.

Why weigh it down with the unnecessary features of other programming languages? He explicitly wanted something easier than the complex tools used for making software programs so that people could easily make web pages. In 1991, the first web server was up and running, and Berners-Lee's colleagues soon made their own web sites and web pages.[18]

In 1993, there were 130 web sites, but within six months, that number more than quadrupled. By 1995, there were over 23,000; the number would continue to double annually.[19] The simplest word processor was all anyone needed to participate, so participate they did—much to Tim Berners-Lee's and the entire world's dismay.

At the time, many computer science experts lamented how slow, un-secure, and immature the technology was behind the World Wide Web. And many still do today. They believe they know better, and that if they could go back in time and tell Berners-Lee or the folks at Netscape—makers of the first commercial web browser—what to do, all those problems would be solved (there certainly would never have been a blink tag).[20] The fallacy is that if they had their wish, they'd end up with an entirely different, and possibly not so successful, World Wide Web. Although the Web is struggling to retrofit privacy, security, and other good things, had they been in place in 1993, they may have raised barriers to entry, slowing or preventing the growth of the Internet we know today.

The factors that spread innovations, from the personal ones listed in Chapter 4 to the broader ones listed above, are largely about ease of adoption. The reason why Internet and cell phone usage climbed faster than previous technologies isn't because things happen faster today. (Nor is it because these technologies are bigger leaps forward than previous ones.) It's simply because the barriers of entry were low. People already had PCs and phone lines, making Internet use cheap and easy (economics). For cellular phones, the population already had daily experience with

---

[18] *http://www.w3.org/People/Berners-Lee/ShortHistory.html* and *http://www.w3.org/History/1989/proposal.html*.

[19] *http://www.mit.edu/people/mkgray/growth/*.

[20] Even the inventor of the blink tag regrets it: *http://en.wikipedia.org/wiki/Blink_tag*.

personal telephone usage and cordless phones, and their frequent use was accepted social behavior (culture). If you think about it, the cell phone isn't more than a cordless phone with unlimited (well, sometimes) range. The Internet and World Wide Web, for all their wonders, were an extension of the PCs and modems already in use—AOL had trained millions to use email, and word processors were popular applications on those computers.

The goodness/adoption paradox surfaces if, for fun, we separate goodness (from the expert's point of view) from the factors that drive adoption (see Figure 8-2). From the expert view of goodness, better technologies existed for publishing and networking than Berners-Lee's Web. Ted Nelson and Doug Engelbart had talked about and demoed them for decades. But those "better" ideas were demanding in ways that would have raised barriers to adoption in 1991. At best, they would have cost more to build and taken more time to engineer. We can't know whether those additional barriers would have prevented the Web from succeeding or merely have changed its ascension. It's also possible these alterative web designs might have had advantages that Berners-Lee's Web didn't have, that would have positively impacted ease of adoption.

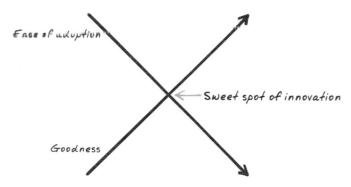

Figure 8-2. *The notion of goodness described by experts often competes with ease of adoption.*

This suggests that the most successful innovations are not the most valuable or the best ideas, but the ones that appear on the sweet spot between what's good from the expert's perspective, and what can be easily adopted, given the uncertainties of all the secondary factors combined. The idealism of goodness and the notion that goodness wins is tempered by the limits and irrationalities of people's willingness to try new things, the culture of the era, and the events of the time. This explains why the first innovators—driven by the complete faith in their ideas—are so often beaten in the market, and in public perception, by latecomers willing to compromise.

CHAPTER 9

Problems and solutions

Living alone in a wooden townhouse miles from London, Isaac
Newton worked endless hours alone by candlelight. Stacks of
papers, journals, and notes from experiments littered the small
manor that was his home. Beyond explaining gravity, inventing
calculus, and revolutionizing science, his true passion—which
fueled his pre-electric age all-nighters—was turning lead into gold.[1]
This 18th-century search for the philosopher's stone—a method
for changing one element into another—occupied many great
minds including Bacon, Boyle, Locke, and Leibniz, and was at the
time believed to be the greatest technological challenge of the age.
One can only guess at how many collective months these most
brilliant minds wasted chasing the impossible. For all his genius,
Newton may as well have been banging his head against the wall
(perhaps preparing him for getting hit by apples), as the laws of
physics we know today render his work an obvious waste of time
(see Figure 9-1).[2]

*Figure 9-1. This painting of Newton, by William Blake, shows him as a
lost hero. Blake felt that Newton's attempts to solve everything through
science and alchemy were misguided.*

---

1 *http://www.pbs.org/wgbh/nova/newton/alch-newman.html.*

2 However, simply because the laws of physics today suggest Newton was wrong
   doesn't mean he was. A breakthrough in our understanding of energy, matter, or
   particle physics could reveal Newton was right about the possibility of the philosopher's stone.

Some say all innovation is a leap of faith, but the sensible (or at least those with mortgage payments) wonder about this: can you know when you're chasing the equivalent of a holy grail, a philosopher's stone, or a perpetual motion machine? Before entrepreneurs and inventors bet their lives on an idea, they want to know that it's achievable. And if it is, do they possess the talents and passions required to make it happen? If Newton, one of the great minds of history, can wander for years down an innovator's dead end, how can a merely bright mind expect to filter the possible from the impossible? The only hope for answers is to look past this mythology—problem solving is not nearly as important as problem finding.

Newton's mistake was the problem he chose, not his methods for solving it. Problem finding—problem solving's shy, freckled, but confident cousin—is the craft of defining challenges so they're easier to solve. Newton's choice set him up to fail before he began, and many bright would-be innovators make similar mistakes: they fail to spend enough time exploring and understanding problems before trying to solve them.

Problems as invitations

The word *problem* often means something bad, as in "Houston, we have a problem" or "I have a problem with your tuna salad," but successful innovation often involves more attention to problems than solutions. Einstein once said, "If I had 20 days to solve a problem, I would take 19 days to define it," a gem of insight lost in the glory of what he achieved on that 20th day. It's counterintuitive because, on the surface, problems rarely need help to be understood. For example, if Bob's pants are covered in flaming napalm, or Jane is being chased by rabid zombie Rottweilers, do they really need to sit and ponder before taking action? In everyday experience, a problem is something we want to get rid of quickly; for example, we know that Bob should rip off his pants, throw them at the Rottweilers, and whisk Jane away, with pants-free charm, for a heroically romantic afternoon.

But the challenges innovators choose have no known solutions or aren't believed to be important at all. No one asked Galileo to explain the solar system, Engelbart to invent the mouse, or Bell to create the telephone. They saw unidentified problems in the world and dedicated themselves to defining and solving them. Einstein's motivation for developing his special theory of relativity, while working as an unknown patent clerk, wasn't that his girlfriend thought it'd be cute. Nor did his boss threaten to fire him if he didn't win the Nobel Prize. Being curious of mind, he followed his own logic and asked questions others were unwilling to ask, and when he saw no answers, he simply set about finding his own.

Discovering problems actually requires just as much creativity as discovering solutions. There are many ways to look at any problem, and realizing a problem is often the first step toward a creative solution. To paraphrase John Dewey, the inventor of the Dewey Decimal System, a properly defined problem is partially solved. And if your particular innovation involves the support of other people, a clearly defined problem helps form bonds and build teams where none existed before. Author John Seely Brown once said, "When we get in the spirit of following a problem to the root, that pursuit of listening to the problem brings multiple disciplines and multiple crafts together. The problem pulls people together."[3]

Framing problems to help solve them

One way to creatively describe a challenge is to compare it to another kind of challenge that's been solved. Scott Cook, the founder of Intuit (makers of Quicken and QuickBooks software), felt that the problem to solve wasn't making good accounting software, but something else entirely: "The greatest competitor…was not in the industry. It was the pencil. The pencil is a tough and resilient substitute. Yet the entire industry had overlooked it."[4] He creatively framed the problem and shifted the perspective of his team to find a better solution than pencil and paper. Even if his competition had more talented problem solvers, engineers, or designers, his creative framing of the problem gave him an advantage. Anyone can use Cook's basic framing strategy; by choosing a powerful reference (the pencil), and framing the challenge around it (sell software), he created opportunities before he wrote a line of code.

---

[3] From an interview in *Breakthrough: Stories and Strategies of Radical Innovation*, by Mark Stefik and Barbara Stefik (MIT Press, 2006).

[4] From *Harvard Business Review on Innovation* (Harvard Business School Press, 2001).

This pattern is everywhere in the history of innovation, but it's often hidden behind tales of brilliance and breakthrough solutions. As a test, follow the trail of any successful innovation far back enough, and odds are high that you'll find a creatively framed problem behind it. While Edison is heralded for the lightbulb, he was late to the party: dozens of other inventors were trying well before he began. His success came from defining the challenge differently. He thought of the lightbulb as a system, asking questions like, "How do you get power to homes to power the lightbulb? And where does that power come from?" A lightbulb alone was useless, and Edison knew why.

Cities had invested millions in gaslights, making any switch to a new technology incredibly expensive—even if there were perfect, cheap lightbulbs for sale. Ever the businessman, Edison was unwilling to make great lightbulbs that no one could buy. The real task to him wasn't "make a working lightbulb," as we're commonly taught. Instead, Edison framed the problem as "make an electricity system cities can use to adopt my lights." It's no surprise his philosophy of invention was based on 1% inspiration and 99% perspiration.[5] With so much confidence in the problems he chose to undertake, he knew it was only a matter of time before he succeed. Edison avoided challenges like the philosopher's stone, or today's (lack of a) grand unified theory of physics, knowing that not enough pieces were in place yet for success to be possible.

A similar story of well-framed problems comes from the rise of personal digital assistants (PDAs). For decades, people talked about handheld devices that could manage your calendar, contacts, and personal information. The 1980s and early 1990s saw HP, Siemens, Sharp, and Apple invest millions in new products, which all failed. It seemed that a successful PDA might be like Newton's philosopher's stone—an impossible task. That was until the Palm Pilot, introduced in 1996, successfully overcame the

---

[5] Tesla, a rival of Edison's—who many believe was a superior inventor—had this to say about Edison's approach to inventing, "If Edison had a needle to find in a haystack, he would proceed at once with the diligence of a bee to examine straw after straw until he found [it]. I was a sorry witness of such doings...a little theory would have saved him ninety percent of his labor." From *The Engines of Our Ingenuity*.

challenges that stumped their competitors; PDAs became a billion dollar industry, influencing the design of computers and mobile phones forever.

The key factor in Palm's success was that they defined their challenge differently than their competitors. Instead of focusing on engineering constraints, or lofty dreams of revolutionizing computers, they focused on what customers wanted. Jeff Hawkins, the founder of Palm, reasoned that his team knew as much about consumer feedback on previous PDAs as their competitors. Why not start the conversation with what people clearly needed, rather than what the companies of the day could provide?

Hawkin's spent an evening at home with a notepad, and soon had the following list of goals for the Pilot project:[6]

- Fits in a shirt pocket
- Syncs seamlessly with PC
- Fast and easy to use
- No more than $299

In 1994, all of these goals were beyond ambitious—they were impossible. If you had shown them to any of the PDA companies of the day, you'd have been told to go home. But Hawkins realized solving these problems was the only real path to success. Handwriting recognition, color displays, or fancy keyboards, were all nice ideas, but they weren't essential. If they could succeed at these four challenges, Hawkins was convinced they had high odds of success.

Look carefully at those four bulleted items: there is great power packed into every one. Notice that the goal wasn't to be small, or handy, but specifically small enough to fit in a shirt pocket. It's an insightful criterion because shirt pockets are a time-tested size for various objects (lighters, cigarette packs, business cards, and most relevant to Palm, calculators), and by framing the challenges in this way, they focused their problem-solving efforts in ways that would pay off. When Hawkins made the list, he didn't know how he'd satisfy those conditions, but the act of spending time framing them was time well spent.

---

6 Andrea Butter and David Pogue, *Piloting Palm: The Inside Story of Palm, Hand-spring, and the Birth of the Billion-Dollar Handheld Industry* (Wiley, 2002), 73.

Other famously innovative projects were based on similar definitions. The book *Blockbusters*, by Gary S. Lynn,[7] examines many
of them and how they came about (see Table 9-1). What's most
interesting is how simple these objectives seem; because of their
clear identification of the problem to solve, they're more powerful
than complex ones. It's hard to forget these simple descriptions, so
they make for useful tests of ideas as they're being developed.

Table 9-1. Famous projects and their goals (from Lynn, except BackPack)

PROJECT	PROBLEM DEFINITIONS/GOALS
Apple IIe	Reduce costs
	Simplify manufacturing
	Modernize
	Look like the Apple II
Original IBM PC	Beat Apple
	Do it in one year
Palm Pilot	Fits in shirt pocket
	Sync with PC
	Fast and easy to use
	Not more than $299
37signals Backpack[1]	Life's loose ends
	Basecamp is overkill
	Pages with simple tools
	Remind me away from the computer

1 Backpack is an innovative web-based organizing tool. Backpack's list was used by
   permission from its creators at *www.37signals.com*.

The Palm Pilot's success came largely from its simplicity as a
product—a quality driven entirely by the self-defined constraints.
In *Piloting Palm*, by Andrea Butter and David Pogue, a book on
the history of the Pilot's development, these criteria enabled decision makers to keep the product so easy to use.

> *Hawkins, who presided over these meetings, was unyielding
> when it came to keeping what he saw as nonessential features out
> of the product. If the new machine were to fail it wouldn't be
> because it had been junked up with unnecessary functions, like its
> predecessors.... Soon the team became experts at killing features.*[8]

---

7 Gary S. Lynn, *Blockbusters* (Collins, 2003).
8 From *Piloting Palm*, 81.

The team's ability to focus on the core constraints—elements necessary for successful innovation—is what made the greatness of the Pilot possible.

Framing the problem by picking strong goals is nothing new: consider the Ten Commandments, the U.S. Bill of Rights, or even the rules for good games. Michael Jordan would never have dunked if James Nesmith had set the height of basketball hoops at 25 feet instead of 10. Hank Aaron wouldn't have hit 755 home runs if the inventors of baseball had decided that a ball hit over the fence was, perhaps most logically, out of bounds. Just like the creative talent of your smartest designer, programmer, or business analyst, picking the right problems to solve and defining them carefully creates a playing field for their talents. It's deceptively hard to create good constraints, and there's less glory in problem finding than solving; however, the number of successful innovations based on clever constraints proves it's worth the time.

Exploring problems with prototypes

If tomorrow at work you found the smartest person in your company sitting at her desk, typing away at a computer, monitor, and mouse all made from wood—without any electronics or working parts of any kind—what would you think? As for the Pilot's development, the true story is that Hawkins designed a wooden model. Early on, after framing the challenge with tough goals, he went to the small shop in his garage and spent hours carving and sawing. Although this wasn't easy, some decisions were straightforward because of the constraints: there were only a handful of ways to design a device to match the criteria. For example, to fit in a shirt pocket, the device could only carry AAA batteries—no other power source known to man could work in that form factor. So, his model assumed AAA. Similar thinking forced decisions about screen size, leading to the choice to go without a keyboard (and Hawkins whittled down a chopstick for use as a makeshift stylus). In a matter of hours, he had a prototype for the Pilot that he brought to work with him the next day.

He carried it around with him to all his meetings, pretending to use it as if it were the finished product. He'd "write" on it, carefully taking it out of his pocket and putting it away, to the dismay of the engineers and marketers on his team. They must have wondered why, for a cutting-edge technology project, their leader would carry around a roughly carved, nonelectronic replica of something that hadn't even been designed yet.

The value to Hawkins was obvious: how else could he explore? He wasn't certain that the problem of "design to fit in a shirt pocket" was the right form factor. It was possible that its shape should be like a banana or perhaps a Rubik's Cube. Or maybe there was another criterion, one they hadn't even imagined, that could only be discovered using the model. To Hawkins, there was no other way. In his words, "An essential part of innovation is to envision the new product or service. You have to use it and experience it before it is designed and built." When dealing with complex problems and many unknowns, innovation happens only when smart ways are found to clarify the challenges.

Anyone who has studied any creative field—painting, engineering, music, writing, and even filmmaking—knows there's nothing new here. Picasso spent hours with preliminary sketches before painting his masterpiece *Les Demoiselles* (he said, "To model an object is to possess it"). The Wright brothers built the first wind tunnel in America just so they could learn more about the airplane prototypes they made. In innovation, there is no alternative; the problems are too large to be attacked in any conventional way.

The truth about serendipity

When Dr. Percy Spencer found a melted candy bar in his shirt pocket while playing with some radar equipment, he had every reason to throw it away. Odds are good that other people in radar laboratories around the world experienced similar globs of chocolate and other foodstuffs in their pockets and did nothing about them, other than to clean up the mess and get back to work. And given that the rational, logical parts of most intelligent people's brains would tell them to do the same (getting rid of the offending savory bits and forgetting about it as soon as possible), it's entirely odd that Spencer chose to do something different. Remember, he essentially found a bit of warm trash in his pocket and decided to spend the rest of the day playing with melted cocoa beans, ignoring the millions of dollars of supercool top-secret defense equipment surrounding him in the lab.

Imagine Spencer in that magical moment: alone in the lab, expensive lights blinking all around, his eyes staring down at two chocolaty fingers, his Hershey-stained clothes and lab coat desperate to be washed. If you walked past him at that instant, you'd think for certain he was insane: a chocolate-fingered loon. But although he didn't know it yet, this chance encounter—the moment that redlined his curiosity well past his logical mind's ability to follow—would lead him to the invention of the microwave oven. Curious about the source of heat, he put some popcorn kernels, and then an egg, by the nearest radar tube. The popcorn popped, and the egg exploded. He quickly found support for more experiments, and he spent the next 10 years developing this chance encounter into one of the most used appliances in the world.

The microwave, Viagra, easy-open soda can, Band-Aids, Nylon, and X-rays were all, as legend has it, discovered by accident. Journalists and teachers are fond of tales of serendipity's grand role in the history of innovation; it's yet another example of the epiphany myth (see Chapter 1). The myth, in this form, is that innovation is random, and that people lucky enough to show up at the right place and at the right time reap rewards. The double-secret hidden message of these tales is that good things can happen to anyone—we're all created equally in our ability to have good fortune knock on our doors. But it's a deception: while serendipity has a starring role in innovation, it's what people do with the chance encounter that matters, and not the chance discovery itself.

In our everyday lives, we encounter odd moments when we see things beyond explanation. Our conditioned response is to ignore these moments or explain them away. We keep going on as planned and pretend we didn't see or think what we thought we did. Yet these moments, for the innovator, are the future knocking on the door. How else will new knowledge appear to us, if not as strange, bizarre, or incomprehensible experiences? (See Chapter 6.) The innovator's response has to be to chase these moments until curiosities are exhausted or new solutions are found, whichever comes first. But for most of us, even in one of these special moments, we fall back to the comfortable illusion that we already know everything there is to know. We forget that the common sense we hold dear today was, years or centuries ago, discovered by an innovative mind willing to ignore the common sense of his own time.

CHAPTER 10

Innovation is always good

*The chief cause of problems
is solutions.*
—Eric Sevareid[1]

In 1903, two crazy young men, without any engineering training or college education, built a machine the world told them couldn't be made. In the frigid 30-mile per hour winds of Kill Devil Hills, a few miles from Kitty Hawk, North Carolina, the Wright brothers made the first sustained powered flight with a person at the controls (see Figure 10-1). Orville won the coin toss and flew first, but the brothers took turns, making four flights before calling it a day. As amazing as their accomplishment was, it went unnoticed: five boys from the nearby village made up most of the crowd. Only two small newspapers bothered to report on the event because it was seen as a stunt, not a technological breakthrough. It's hard to believe, but the Wright brothers landed their plane on a not very interested planet. The world would have to wait another 30 years for the commercial aviation industry to begin.

Figure 10-1. *An early Wright brothers' glider on a test run at the famed Kill Devil Hills.*

But the most curious thing about the development of powered flight wasn't the world's lack of interest in the Wright brothers' ideas: it was their pitch to potential investors. They didn't talk about multibillion dollar industries, revolutionizing travel across the planet, or connecting people around the world. Instead, their pitch centered on the most ambitious idea in the history of civilization: the end of war.[2] They imagined that their small aircraft, in

---

1 *http://www.museum.tv/archives/etv/S/htmlS/sevareideri/sevareideri.htm.*

2 *http://www.archives.gov/publications/prologue/2003/winter/aero-conference-1. html.*

the hands of democratic governments, could be used to observe enemy movements from afar, rendering surprise attacks and violent conflicts useless.[3] The Wrights spent six years pitching their idea to the governments of the U.S., France, Germany, and Great Britain, eventually selling an aircraft to the U.S in 1909.

Despite the wonders the airplane delivered to civilization, revolutionizing travel, commerce, and communication, it must have been tragic for Orville Wright to live through not one, but two World Wars with significant and strategic roles for aircraft. WWII saw the German Blitzkrieg, the U.S. fire bombings of Dresden (where hundreds of thousands of civilians were killed), and the only wartime uses of atomic bombs in history, all horrific events made possible by airplanes born of the Wrights' design.[4] Airplanes revolutionized warfare, changing forever the power balance of world politics in favor of those with superior air forces. And as the terrorist attacks on New York City on 9/11 revealed yet again, the uses of innovations like airplanes are impossible to predict.

In our religions, histories, and mythologies, we hold innovators to be great heroes, but we rarely speak their names when the downsides of their creations arise. In popular Greek mythology, the god Prometheus was loved for bringing fire to mankind, but shouldn't he also be partially accountable for the burning of Rome? Or, on a more personal level, if I gave you an apple pie that tasted good but later made you ill, wouldn't you complain? What if you bought a machine that saved you time but stained your clothes? Or a drink that doubled your efficiency but caused insomnia? It's overlooked by most, but some mythologies fear innovators. Prometheus, who brought fire to mankind, was chained to a rock and tortured for eternity (see Figure 10-2). The men who tried to build the Tower of Babel in the biblical book *Genesis* were cursed and divided across the world.

---

[3] This belief in technology, particularly weaponry, as ending war, was shared by the inventors of dynamite and the submarine. Tesla also built war machines with this ideal in mind. The telegraph, television, the Internet, and even neural implants have been heralded with the same war-ending powers. An observer of history might note the problems that lead to war seem to have nothing to do with technology and much to do with human nature.

[4] Einstein, whose $E=mc^2$ played a pivotal role in the creation of nuclear weapons, agonized over the moral challenges involved with the use of his discoveries. See *http://www.amnh.org/exhibitions/einstein/peace/manhattan.php*.

Figure 10-2. *Rubens' famous painting of Prometheus Bound. In the myth, Prometheus is chained to a rock, and every day an eagle comes and eats his liver, which regenerates by the next day. In most mythologies, there is a price for innovation. Prometheus Bound was also the subtitle of Mary Shelly's Frankenstein.*

The invention of the airplane certainly worked out well, especially if your last name is Boeing or you're a pilot. But what if, instead, you are the railroad mogul ruined by air travel's rise, or an honest family man who witnessed the destruction of your home by bombs dropped from airplanes? It's a different story. As we'll see, sorting out the meaning and impact of innovations is more complex than the task of making the innovations themselves.

Measuring innovation: the goodness scale

We all think we know what good is, but like all definitions, its shine fades when applied to real life. What might be good for you, finding a thousand dollars in your underwear or waking up on a Maui beach, is probably bad for someone or something else (the person who lost the money, and the hapless sand crabs crushed beneath you). What we casually call *good* is never beneficial to everyone: it depends on who you are and where you stand. As Shakespeare wrote, "There is nothing either good or bad, but thinking makes it so," and our diverse thinking on goodness is reflected by the 50 or more definitions for the word *good* offered by most dictionaries.

The same goes for innovation. Is an innovation good if it solves your problems or makes you money? Definitely. But what if it also causes people to lose their jobs? Or, as is more often the case, what if after people spend days learning to use the innovation, there is little benefit? Or their lives are more complicated? And then consider plastics, typewriters, and televisions, innovations that have brought many good things to the world. But what of the 2-liter soda bottles resting forever in landfills, the typewriters that were used to schedule trains to Auschwitz, or the millions of children watching hours of adult television in lieu of day care? Can we call these, and others like them, innovations because they're good in the largest sense? And, despite all the positive revolutions they've brought to the world, personal computers leave a wake of toxins and chemicals behind every time they're replaced by newer machines.[5]

There's no easy answer to this examination of innovation goodness, leaving plenty of room, much like the previous chapter, for the mythology of "all innovation is good" to survive. We have so much history with innovation as the driving force for our culture, economy, and psychology—from the cotton gin and Industrial Revolution to the personal computer and the Internet Age—that our confidence in innovation approximates a faith; when in doubt, innovate, despite the growing wave of unanswered questions about innovations past.

But there is at least one truth: all innovations combine good and bad effects regardless of the intention of the innovator or how well designed they are.[6] If we accept this, and concede that perspective is everything when it comes to goodness, we can reframe our judgment of innovations.

---

5 *http://www.greenpeace.org/international/news/green-electronics-guide-ewaste250806.*
6 Certainly some creators can steer their creations one way or another. The inventor of a drug that cures stupidity or converts assholes into saints would be hard to criticize. Some inventors are agnostic about how their work is used, but in the cases of OXO good grips or prosthetic limb designers, there is definitely a goodness factor in how the thing itself is designed and the problems it intends to solve.

An innovation can be:

- **Good for you.** The innovation earns you money, is enjoyable to work on, or solves a problem that interests you.

- **Good for others.** The innovation provides income to help family and friends; solves problems for the poor, sick, or needy; or through the innovation, or profits generated from it, improves the lives of people other than you.

- **Good for an industry or economy.** The innovation has benefits for many businesses and creates new opportunities for at least a subset of an industry or economy. Disruptions caused by the innovation are outweighed by new opportunities created.

- **Good for a society.** The innovation has a net positive effect on a community, city, state, or nation. While there might be some negative uses of the innovation, the net effect is overwhelmingly positive. The innovation is designed for sustained value, not just short term. The innovator identified who it might be bad for and tried to minimize those effects.

- **Good for the world.** The innovation has a net positive on the future of the human race.

And we can also ask the twin questions:

- What problems does this innovation solve? Whose problems are they?

- What problems does this innovation create? Whose problems are they?

This list shows that many famous innovators can at best claim to have made things good for them, or good for corporations, with little value for others. (Having a large IPO or selling ideas for millions has debatable value on the goodness scale.) And many popular innovations—such as lightbulbs, automobiles, and computers—definitely benefit individuals and industries, but their contributions are tarnished by their negative environmental impacts. It gets complex quickly, but by framing the value of innovations on different perspectives, understanding innovation becomes possible. The biases or self-interests that limit definitions of goodness are forced to surface.

Innovations are unpredictable (DDT, automobiles, and the Internet)

An illustrative tale of the challenge of goodness starts with a mix of chemicals, a Swiss scientist, and hordes of disease-carrying insects. In 1948, to the despair of mosquitoes everywhere, Paul Muller recognized the bug-killing properties of dichloro-diphenyl-trichloroethane, commonly known as DDT. This chemical was the first true pesticide in history and was used in enormous quantities during WWII to control the spread of typhus and malaria. It was so successful that in 1955 the World Health Organization (WHO) proudly armed with DDT, planned to eliminate malaria from the planet. The belief was that DDT's supreme potency, lasting for years in soil and weeks in water, could permanently eliminate disease-carrying insects in infested areas.

But the WHO soon observed strange things in places where DDT was used. Scientists realized that this new chemical had unexpected and complex collateral effects. The story went like this:

> The mosquitoes were effectively eliminated; however roaches, less sensitive to DDT, survived, absorbing the poison. Small lizards happily ate the roaches. Those lizards developed nerve damage from the DDT (providing the widowed roaches with bittersweet glee), who, in their slow, near-drunken stupor, were easily consumed en masse by the local cat population. The cats, more sensitive to the DDT than the lizards, died by the thousands, opening the door for an explosion in the rat population. And the kicker to the whole sordid tale is that the rats brought the threat of the plague to humans.[7]

For all their confidence, the technological leaders of the world were dumbfounded by the chain of events their actions put into play. At first, the WHO and many scientists refused to believe that DDT could be responsible for everything they observed. It was unimaginable to the best scientific minds of the 1950s that one little chemical could cause so much damage. And since DDT was

---

[7] This is a careful combination of several different accounts. There are many secondary reports that provide similar, and in some cases, more dramatic tellings of the events. See http://www.sfgate.com/cgi-bin/article.cgi?file=/chronicle/archive/2003/12/13/HOGK63KAVL1.DTL and http://www.cdra.org.za/creativity/Parachuting%20cats%20into%20Borneo.htm.

so new, and there were no mass uses of chemicals like DDT on record, everyone was ignorant of the possibilities. Much like the major innovations of the last decades—cell phones, wireless Internet, personal computers—DDT changed so much about how things worked that it was impossible to predict its impact, positive and negative, before it was used (see Figure 10-3).

Figure 10-3. *DDT and airplanes were a perfect match. Here, DDT is being used on cattle to give them extra special flavor.*

Before DDT, people had little reason to fear pesticides or chemicals of any kind. It wasn't until Rachel Carson's book, *Silent Spring*, that people became aware of the negative impacts of DDT, and the modern environmental movement was born.[8] Beforehand, there was little public knowledge about the possibility of chemicals moving up the food chain, or the unpredictable nature of shifting the species' balance in ecosystems. The science community did not understand the interconnectedness of ecologies and

---

[8] There are still debates about the true risks of DDT, the Borneo tale, and whether the studies done of DDT on birds were accurate. Regardless of how much of this particular truth we surface, my point holds steady: all innovations have unpredictable effects, both good and bad. And often, as perhaps in the case of DDT, it takes a long time to understand the true impact of an innovation. See *http://reason.com/rb/rb061202.shtml.*

had little experience with the new kinds of chemicals they were producing. DDT's greatest value was its staying power, yet it was nearly impossible to predict that this very property would have intense destructive effects.

Other major innovations show similar patterns of diffusion with unexpected consequences arising as a result of successful adoption. Automobiles are one of the great successes of the early 20th century. They revolutionized society, enabling unprecedented commerce, travel, and leisure for the middle classes around the world. But their success has created many sizable, perhaps inescapable problems; for example, over one million people are killed annually in automobile accidents (nearly 40,000 in the U.S. alone). Automobiles require expensive road development and upkeep, and they are major contributors to pollution (see Table 10-1).

Table 10-1. The two sides of innovations

Innovation	Good effects	Bad effects
DDT	Controlled malaria, elevated living conditions in third-world nations, inspired professional Wrestling move[1]	Disturbed ecology, collateral species impact, DDT-resistant mosquitoes evolved
Automobile	Personalized transportation, empowered individuals, boosted commerce and urban development	Creates half of pollution in urban areas, 40,000 annual U.S. fatalities, traffic, gave birth to suburbs[2]
Personal computers	Individual empowerment, communication, learning, the Internet	Rate of upgrades creates landfill, production uses and creates hazardous materials[3]
Cell phones	Wireless communication, mobile access, convenience, portable emergency and safety system	Public annoyance, bad drivers become unguided missiles, that annoying person next to you in a restaurant

[1] *http://en.wikipedia.org/wiki/DDT_(professional_wrestling).*
[2] *http://www.who.int/world-health-day/2004/infomaterials/world_report/en/.*
[3] *http://update.unu.edu/archive/issue31_5.htm.*

This is an essential paradox of innovation: no one knows, not even the inventors, how their creations will impact the world until they are used. Ford did not imagine pizza delivery boys. The McDonald brothers didn't imagine epidemic obesity. Bill Gates and Steve Jobs did not consider software viruses. And Gutenberg, with all of his bibles, didn't envision *The Da Vinci Code*, nor the *New York Times* bestseller list it disgracefully (at least to him—he was printing bibles after all) dominated for months. For all the wishful thinking of innovators, innovations always have unintended consequences. They are free for use by others, and because everyone has different needs, values, idea, and desires, there's no telling how the innovations born of one mind will be used by another.

A popular opinion held among inventors is that true breakthrough ideas are so different from our current thinking that we have no idea how to use them. This means that not only is the use of an innovation unpredictable after it has been accepted, but the time and motivation for its acceptance is unpredictable as well. Gordon Gould, one the inventors of the Laser, said:

> The triode...was invented in 1910, but it took years before a vacuum tube was ever sold commercially. Nobody knew what to do with them. They just knew that a triode provided a wonderful way to control a current with an electrical signal instead of a mechanical switch. Like the triode, the laser is also very basic and important invention. But for the first five years or so of its life, there was a saying that the laser was "a solution in search of a problem."9

Many researchers take pride in this uncertainty, as it proves that they are as far out as possible in front of what we know, satisfying their drive to work in territory where breakthroughs are possible. But they downplay their lack of control, or their concerns, for how their discovery will be used. The intention of goodness doesn't bind the movement of ideas in any way. Barbed wire, designed to control cattle, which had innocent intentions (well, unless you're a cow), found its way into a pivotal role in WWI, limiting soldiers' movement across trenches and enabling some of

---

9 From *Inventors at Work: Interviews with 16 Notable American Inventors.*

the bloodiest warfare in the history of mankind.[10] Einstein's theory of relativity revolutionized our understanding of the universe, but despite Einstein's initial disapproval, led to the atomic bomb. From every wonder comes a horror, and no one can claim certainty over what future the pursuit of an innovation will create.

To be fair, the movement of innovation works the other way just as easily. Technologies developed for warfare—including the Jeep automobile, MedEvac helicopters, jet aircraft, trench coats, and microwave ovens—often find important commercial, mass-market, and humanitarian uses.[11] Even the technologies used to develop the Internet originated in U.S. Government defense projects and with government funding. Guerilla warfare inspired guerilla marketing, and on it goes. The lesson is that morality, or any philosophy, is invisible to the forces of innovation, and any innovator who takes his work seriously must operate with this in mind.

Technology accelerates without discrimination

Imagine an innovation that cut your travel time to work in half. Impossible? One breakthrough of the 19th century was the clipper sailboat. Larger, faster, and more maneuverable, it reinvented cross-Atlantic trade and revolutionized the economies of entire nations. Until the 1830s, it took five weeks to make the crossing, but the Clipper could do it in 12 days. It was a great innovation, accelerating many good things, but some bad ones as well.

In 1845, the Great Potato Famine began in Ireland, leading to the death of hundreds of thousands of people. It's believed that the potato fungus that destroyed Ireland's crops came from North America.[12] One theory is that the famine hadn't occurred sooner because the five-week journey across the Atlantic was long enough for the fungus to die in transit. However, the shorter 12-day itinerary left the fungus alive, so it was only a matter if time

---

[10] http://en.wikipedia.org/wiki/Trench_warfare.

[11] http://abcnews.go.com/GMA/Technology/story?id=1796227.

[12] They're still sorting this out, but one report claims the infested potato came from Mexico: http://www.pnas.org/cgi/content/abstract/91/24/11591.

before it infested the clipper's destination.[13] There were other major causes, political and economical, but had the innovation of the clipper ship not taken place, the Great Famine might never have happened.

Most innovations have similar stories. Personal computers, which can be programmed to do anything, created the possibility of computer viruses. The Internet, designed to accelerate and distribute information, hastened the spread of those viruses, as well as spam, scams, and misinformation. Automobiles speed the police to crime scenes, but they also help thieves get away. The rising tide of technology raises all boats.

Instant messages and cell phone conversations are innovations in conveyance, as are many technological innovations. But they have no impact on the quality of the messages themselves, just as high-resolution television sets have zero effect on the quality of the acting or writing in the shows. Unless you're developing an innovation that motivates people to communicate more clearly or less selfishly, innovations that accelerate are unlikely to change the world in the way their creators expect. If you have someone good to talk to, and something important to talk about, communication is rarely in need of acceleration. In fact, software that rewards people for slowing down and thinking about what they're reading and writing might be the greatest innovation of our time.

The good and bad, the future and the past

Where I grew up in New York City, sailboats were a mystery. My heart was with highways, subways, and rockets. On the days I'd happen to see a sail in Long Island Sound, I wondered why anyone would choose to travel slower than the latest technology allowed. But my opinion changed the first time I traveled on one. Standing in the shade of the sail, watching the smooth wooden bow rise with the waves, I felt the quiet power of the wind move me. Friends talked and calmly watched the sea, instead of fighting the roar and stink of diesel. The sails opened like wings, and we flew over the waves, the spines in the sail shining in engineered elegance, like the cable spans of the Brooklyn Bridge, providing an experience that no powerboat of any speed could ever replace.

---

[13] From *Diffusion of Innovations*, 452.

Many innovations, for all their progress, leave a sailboat of forgotten goodness behind. And in our race to innovate, we instinctively reject people who hold on to the past. We can't know that they don't have a point. Perhaps they've pointed out something timeless that we didn't think about. Is there an innovation that can replace a hug from your mom? Ice cream on a summer day? Is a strip mall a worthy substitute for an open meadow, or the latest Gehry office tower for the Chrysler Building? The passion of creation leaves us partially blind; we're focused so intently on what we're making that we forget the good things already here, or that our innovations might leave behind.

And while we laugh at groups who reject innovation as a concept—the Luddites, the Amish, or our technophobic friends—we are all just as resistant as they are, but in different ways. We follow conventions in our dress, speech, diets, and work schedules. We drive on the same side of the road, put socks on before our shoes, and eat dinner with knives and forks. Even the greatest innovators of all time, the big revolutionaries and radicals, followed the traditions of their day. No one innovates in all ways all the time; in fact, the biggest, baddest innovators in history followed more conventions than they broke.

As social creatures, we depend on traditions to form communities, governments, and families, and we believe these traditions are important enough to justify sacrificing our lives, or the lives of others, to protect them from change. And the grand irony is that all traditions, even religious ones, began as innovations. There was a day before men wore suits, and a time before Jews, Christians, and Muslims had their first holy texts (or the first churches to pray in). All of these ideas evolved into traditions over time, but only because people were, one day, willing (or forced) to try something new. There's a circular nature to innovation that's hard to see, but we're living inside it all the time.

The best philosophy of innovation is to accept both change and tradition and to avoid the traps of absolutes. As ridiculous as it is to accept all new ideas simply because they're new, it's equally silly to accept all traditions simply because they're traditions. Ideas new and old have their place in the future, and it's our job to put them there.

Research and recommendations

This is fuel for the curious: I've provided copious notes for anyone seeking more knowledge about the preceding topics. There are two bibliographies—one annotated, the other ranked—and a summary of other research used to support the writing of this book. Good luck; let me know what gems you find.

Annotated bibliography

Myths and mythology

Campbell, Joseph and Bill Moyers. *The Power of Myth*. Anchor, 1991.

> The most accessible book in the Joseph Campbell cannon. It's a set of interviews conducted by Bill Moyers and covers many of the major themes in Campbell's other works. Of prime importance is that this text explains why myths matter, how they function, and their relevance to today's challenges. If you like this one, follow up with Campbell's *Myths to Live By* (Souvenir Press Ltd, 1995).

Armstrong, Karen. *A Short History of Myths*. Canongate, 2005.

> This short book follows the history of myths from the beginnings of creation myths to the modern age. Armstrong is a master at approaching the subject of belief in an informal yet scholarly way, and she provides an excellent counterpoint to *The Power of Myth*. Both books avoid getting into pantheons or comparative mythology, but plant seeds for why you'd want to go there.

Businness innovation

Drucker, Peter. *Innovation and Entrepreneurship*. Collins, 1993.

> A star in my research. His approach is wise and concise, he writes well, and he uses stories more than statistics to support claims. If you want to understand the business of innovation or are interested in start-up ventures, this is a must-read.

Hargadon, Andrew. *How Breakthroughs Happen: The Surprising Truth About How Companies Innovate*. Harvard Business School Press, 2003.

Hargadon touches on many themes found in my research, and he emphasizes interesting stories from history over charts and statistics. My only regret is that I didn't find this book earlier.

Foster, Richard. *Innovation: The Attacker's Advantage*. Simon & Schuster, 1988.

As best I can tell, this is the first book that uses the S curve of innovation, a model reused in many modern business books. There's often value in returning to the source of ideas, and Foster does not disappoint. Unlike the two books listed previously, this book is largely about strategy and tactics, but it also provides the reasons, based on history, that those tactics work.

Kawasaki, Guy. *The Art of the Start: The Time-Tested, Battle-Hardened Guide for Anyone Starting Anything*. Portfolio, 2004.

With this title, you know the author knows marketing. This short book is thin on history or theory, but is full of action, motivation, and guts. It's the antidote to the ever-present innovation killer of too much thinking and not enough doing.

Creative thinking and problem solving

Csikszentmihalyi, Mihaly. *Creativity: Flow and the Psychology of Discovery and Invention*. HarperPerennial, 1997.

He's a master of creativity research, and this book is my favorite of his works. It's based on a long-term study of many creative minds, examining their points of view on how creativity happens. His research provided the clearest description of the processes described in Chapter 1.

From the Earth to the Moon, Episode 5: Spider, HBO, 1998.

This is part five of an excellent dramatization of the NASA race to the moon. This episode focuses on the design of the lunar lander: a fantastic story of politics, ignored ideas, creative problem solving, collaboration, and dozens of other topics. Highly recommended: watch it with your coworkers and compare and contrast. This is an excellent companion to the film *Apollo 13*.

Brown, Kenneth A. *Inventors at Work: Interviews with 16 Notable American Inventors*. Microsoft Press, 1988.

This is a series of interviews with great inventors of the 20th century and is a companion to *Programmers at Work*, from the same publisher. If you want to innovate, the best bet is to listen to those who do it, talking about how it's done; this collection hits on many great themes and stories. Forget "how to be creative" books—read these guys and then get to work. (Also see Jessica Livingston's *Founders at Work: Stories of Startups' Early Days*, Apress, 2007.)

Stone, Irving. *The Agony and the Ecstasy*. NAL Trade, 2004.

Historic fiction can be tough, but this one gets it right. It's the life of Michelangelo written as a novel, but based on extensive research. This book is highly recommended for high-minded innovators. Michelangelo was one of the greats, and the details of his life—especially his resistance to the powers of the day—will put fire in your heart. There is a 1965 film of the same name, but read the book first. The film stars Charlton Heston and doesn't have the same insights for would-be innovators as the book (but it is a fun watch over beers with sarcastic artists and creatives).

Flatow, Ira. *They All Laughed*. HarperCollins, 1992.

This book is a series of short pieces about how many great inventions came to be, including television, Teflon, copy machines, Vaseline, and Silly Putty. Flatow's angle is drama and suffering, as all of these stories are unexpectedly complicated, difficult, and frustrating (for the inventors, not the readers). It's not deep history, and there are some shortcuts of accuracy, but it's highly accessible, thought provoking, and humbling.

History and culture

Loewen, James W. *Lies My Teacher Told Me.* Touchstone, 1996.
Zinn, Howard. *A People's History of the United States.* Harper-Collins, 1980.

It takes courage to surface truths that have been paved over for decades, and both of these books take that challenge head on. Loewen's book, focused on an analysis of American school textbooks, is worth the price for its retelling of Thanksgiving alone; Zinn's work, more politically minded, will close the distance between how Americans see themselves compared to how the world sees them. Both are worldview-shifting books.

Carr, Edward Hallett. *What Is History?* Vintage, 1967.

Books that blow your mind in 200 pages deserve special praise: this is one of them. Some others in the field of historiography find this book too dramatic and provocative, but it worked for me, showing me the big questions that historians are supposed to ask and making me interested in the answers.

Pacey, Arnold. *The Maze of Ingenuity.* MIT Press, 1992.

Pacey's aim is to show the parallels between innovation today and Western innovations over the centuries, including an emphasis on how cultures at different times perceived the value of their works. It's a short, dense book, but if you like surprises about how old technologies were made, you'll enjoy and remember it.

Rogers, Everett M. *Diffusion of Innovations.* Free Press, 1995.

As mentioned earlier, this anthropological approach to understanding innovation was compelling and influential. The book is long and academic in style, but the stories are so good that you won't mind. Skipping around is OK because the main points are established early and referenced throughout.

Ranked bibliography

Traditional bibliographies provide little value. They obscure the relative value of prior works and ignore how the author used them (were they devoured, skimmed, or used as a paperweight?). In addition to the annotated bibliography, I experimented with different formats for a comprehensive listing, and the result is this ranked bibliography. The intention is to indicate which sources drew attention during research.

The order below is based on a review of more than 200 pages of my research notes. Every note I took from a book counted as one point and the references are listed in ranked order. There is no ideal system for ranking influence (the flaw in this one is that not all notes influenced me equally), but this was the best of all those suggested.

82, *Innovation and Entrepreneurship*, Peter Drucker

67, *How Breakthroughs Happen: The Surprising Truth About How Companies Innovate*, Andrew Hargadon

55, *Diffusion of Innovations*, Everett M. Rogers

55, *The Engines of Our Ingenuity*, John Lienhard

52, *Creativity in Science: Chance, Logic, Genius, and Zeitgeist*, Dean Keith Simonton

50, *Fire in the Crucible: The Alchemy of Creative Genius*, John Briggs

49, *The Grace of Great Things: Creativity and Innovation*, Robert Grudin

46, *Really Useful: The Origins of Everyday Things*, Joel Levy

46, *Breakthrough: Stories and Strategies of Radical Innovation*, Mark Stefik and Barbara Stefik

44, *Innovation: The Basis for Cultural Change*, H. G. Barnett

36, *The Maze of Ingenuity*, Arnold Pacey

35, *Beethoven: The Universal Composer*, Edmund Morris

34, *Creativity: Beyond the Myth of Genius*, Robert W. Weisberg

33, *The Evolution of Technology*, George Basalla

32, *Mastering the Dynamics of Innovation*, James Utterback

30, *Sparks of Genius*, Robert S. Root-Bernstein and Michele M. Root-Bernstein

28, *Connections*, James Burke

27, *What Is History?*, Edward Hallett Carr

26, *Innovation Paradox: The Success of Failure, the Failure of Success*, Richard Farson and Ralph Keyes

24, *A Brief History of the Future*, John Naughton

23, *The Company: A Short History of a Revolutionary Idea*, John Micklethwait and Adrian Wooldridge

22, *Isaac Newton*, James Gleick

22, *Philosophy of History*, Paul Newall (*http://galilean-library. org/int18.html*)

22, *Innovation: The Attacker's Advantage*, Richard Foster

21, *Inventors at Work: Interviews with 16 Notable American Inventors*, Kenneth A. Brown

21, *Applied Imagination*, Alex F. Osborn

20, *Future Hype: The Myths of Technology Change*, Bob Seidensticker

19, *Fumbling the Future: How Xerox Invented, Then Ignored, the First Personal Computer*, Douglas K. Smith and Robert C. Alexander

19, *Medici Effect: What Elephants and Epidemics Can Teach Us About Innovation*, Frans Johansson

18, *How We Got Here: A Slightly Irreverent History of Technology and Markets*, Andy Kessler

17, *They All Laughed*, Ira Flatow

17, *Gutenberg: How One Man Remade the World with Words*, John Man

16, *A Short History of Myths*, Karen Armstrong

16, *The Innovators: The Discoveries, Inventions, and Breakthroughs of Our Time*, John Diebold

16, *The Big Idea*, Steven D. Strauss

16, *Origins of Genius: Darwinian Perspectives on Creativity*, Dean Keith Simonton

16, *The Victorian Internet*, Tom Standage

15, *Innovation: Driving Product, Process, and Market Change*, Edward B. Roberts

14, *Bootstrapping: Douglas Engelbart, Coevolution, and the Origins of Personal Computing*, Thierry Bardini

14, *Myth: Biography of Belief*, David Leeming

12, *Lucky or Smart*, Bo Peabody

12, *Creativity: Flow and the Psychology of Discovery and Invention*, Mihaly Csikszentmihalyi

12, *The Progress Paradox: How Life Gets Better While People Feel Worse*, Gregg Easterbrook

12, *The Creative Habit: Learn It and Use It for Life*, Twyla Tharp

12, *The Innovator's Solution: Creating and Sustaining Successful Growth*, Clayton M. Christensen

11, *Lost Discoveries*, Dick Teresi

11, *The Art of the Start: The Time-Tested, Battle-Hardened Guide for Anyone Starting Anything*, Guy Kawasaki

11, *Amazon.com: Get Big Fast*, Robert Spector

11, *Eurekas and Euphorias: The Oxford Book of Scientific Anecdotes*, Walter Gratzer

10, *National Geographic Book of Inventions*, Ian Harrison

10, *Blink*, Malcolm Gladwell

10, *Visions of Technology*, Richard Rhodes

10, *The Google Story*, David A. Vise

10, *Alexander the Great's Art of Strategy*, Partha Bose

10, *Technological Innovation: A Critical Review of Current Knowledge*, Patrick Kelly and Melvin Kranzberg

9, *Organizing Genius: The Secrets of Creative Collaboration*, Warren Bennis and Patricia Ward Biederman

9, *The Art of Innovation*, Tom Kelley et al.

9, *Blockbusters*, Gary S. Lynn

9, *Harvard Business Review on Innovation*, Clayton M. Christensen et al.

9, *Managing Creativity and Innovation*, Harvard Business Essentials

8, *Ten Theories of Human Nature*, Leslie Steveson and David L. Haberman

8, *Juice: The Creative Fuel That Drives World-Class Inventors*, Evan I. Schwartz

8, *The Wisdom of Crowds*, James Surowiecki

8, *The Change Function: Why Some Technologies Take Off and Others Crash and Burn*, Pip Coburn

8, *The Act of Creation*, Arthur Koestler

8, *Founders at Work: Stories of Startups' Early Days*, Jessica Livingston

8, *Sciences of the Artificial*, Herbert A. Simon

7, *Forbes' Greatest Business Stories of All Time*, Daniel Gross

7, *Salt: A World History*, Mark Kurlansky

7, *One Good Turn: A Natural History of the Screwdriver and the Screw*, Witold Rybczynski

6, *Higher: A Historic Race to the Sky and the Making of a City*, Neal Bascomb

6, *We Reach the Moon: The Story of Man's Greatest Adventure*, John Noble Wilford

6, *The Search: How Google and Its Rivals Rewrote the Rules of Business and Transformed Our Culture*, John Battelle

6, *Dealing with Darwin: How Great Companies Innovate at Every Phase of Their Evolution*, Geoffrey A. Moore

6, *Just for Fun: The Story of an Accidental Revolutionary*, Linus Torvolds and David Diamond

6, *Industrial Creativity: The Psychology of the Inventor*, Joseph Rossman

5, Wikipedia: Scientific method

5, *Innovation: The Missing Dimension*, Richard K. Lester and Michael J. Piore

4, *The Perfect Thing: How the iPod Shuffles Commerce, Culture, and Coolness*, Steven Levy

4, *Invention by Design: How Engineers Get from Thought to Thing*, Henry Petroski

4, *The Private Life of a Masterpiece*, Monica Bohm-Duchen

4, Wikipedia: Gutenberg

4, *The Structure of Scientific Revolutions*, Thomas S. Kuhn

4, *Mavericks!*, Don Blohowiak

4, *The Eurkea Effect: The Art and Logic of Breakthrough Thinking*, David Perkins

3, *Creativity in Business*, Michael Ray and Rochelle Myers

3, *The Map of Innovation: Creating Something Out of Nothing*, Kevin O'Connor and Paul B. Brown

3, *Innovation at the Speed of Laughter: 8 Secrets to World-Class Idea Generation*, John Sweeny

3, *Revolution in Science*, I. Bernard Cohen

2, *Dealers of Lightning: Xerox PARC and the Dawn of the Computer Age*, Michael Hiltzik

2, *The Sociology of Invention*, S.C. Gilfillan

1, *The Perfect Store: Inside eBay*, Adam Cohen

1, *The Future of Ideas: The Fate of the Commons in a Connected World*, Lawrence Lessig

1, *Of Innovations*, Francis Bacon (*http://oregonstate.edu/instruct/phl302/texts/bacon/bacon_essays.html*)

1, *Cracking Creativity: The Secrets of Creative Genius*, Michael Michalko

1, *When Old Technologies Were New*, Carolyn Marvin

1, *Mavericks at Work: Why the Most Original Minds in Business Win*, William C. Taylor and Polly G. LaBarre

0, *The Art of Project Management*, Scott Berkun

Other research sources

- **Interviews.** Over the course of two years, I interviewed more than 100 people, ranging from phone/email conversations to serendipitous airplane and bus chitchat, and all the way to conference room debates and multi-hour beer-enhanced discussions. These conversations were a primary source of inspiration for sorting out which myths to cover and the most useful angle of exploration for each one. Interviews are the only way to access true stories of innovation too graphic, embarrassing, absurd, or criminal to ever find their way on the record.

- **Lectures and discussion.** Some of the book's themes were presented in lectures at Google, Microsoft, Amazon.com, Adaptive Path MX, Seattle Mindcamp, O'Reilly's FOO camp and Ignite, University of Washington, and MIT. I'm grateful for all those who asked questions, pointed out mistakes, and laughed at my jokes.

- **Web site.** As an experiment, I used my web site to raise questions, ask for references, propose hypotheses for feedback, and extend the reach of my research. It proved a fantastic way to benefit from people I'd never have access to otherwise.

- **Survey.** 110 people who identified themselves as innovators filled out an online questionnaire exploring both general innovation and innovation mythology. These people ranked from scientists to writers to computer programmers to artists. This survey was intended to provide anecdotal evidence, and the results are not of a rigor to infer much beyond what was mentioned in Chapter 6. Selections of the results can be found at *http://www.scottberkun.com/blog/?p=422.*

Photo credits

Chapter openers

Preface, New York, NY, U.S., Yann Le Coroller (*http://www.kub. fr/photos/*)

Chapter 1, Taken at Langeoog, Germany, Lothar Knopp (*http:// www.flickr.com/photos/lotse*)

Chapter 2, Paris, France, Frank Lee (*www.flee.com*)

Chapter 3, Highway 9 in Santa Cruz, CA, U.S., Chuck Rogers (*http://www.flickr.com/photos/two-wrongs/*)

Chapter 4, David's Seattle apartment, David Adam-Edelstein (*http://www.noise-to-signal.com/*)

Chapter 5, Melbourne, Australia, James Robertson (*http://www. flickr.com/photos/shingen_au/*)

Chapter 6, Melbourne, Australia, James Robertson (*http://www. flickr.com/photos/shingen_au/*)

Chapter 7, Lijiang, China, Fillip Forte (*http://flickr.com/photos/ fortes/*)

Chapter 8, Taken at Sanssouci, Potsdam, Germany, Lothar Knopp (*http://www.flickr.com/photos/lotse*)

Chapter 9, Texas, U.S., Robin Walker (*http://www.pbase.com/ walk1*)

Chapter 10, Langeoog, Germany, Lothar Knopp (*http://www. flickr.com/photos/lotse*)

Appendix, James Hague (*http://www.flickr.com/photos/jhague/*)

Figures

Figure 2-2, Photograph by Maria Kaloudi

Figure 3-1, Photograph by Liam Abrahamsen

Figure 4-1, Photograph by Jimmy Wewer

Figure 8-1, Courtesy NASA/JPL-CalTech

Figure 9-1, ©Tate, London 2007

Figure 10-2, W1950-3-1, Rubens, Peter Paul; *Prometheus Bound*; Philadelphia Museum of Art: Purchased with the W/P. Wilstach Collection, 1950

Figure 10-3, AP/WIDE WORLD PHOTOS

Acknowledgments

To Jill: for 16 years of everything.

Mary O'Brien, my editor, for having the courage to say yes, for earning my trust, and for leaving me just enough alone.

Marlowe Shaeffer, friend and rock-star production editor extraordinaire, and the book team of Kate Basart (cover), Rob Romano (illustrations), Ron Bilodeau (interior design), Caitrin McCullough (editorial), Sara Peyton (PR), Steve Fehler (Creative Director), Reba Libby (proofreader), and Ellen Troutman (indexer).

The quiet of many 2 a.m. nights and the crazy owls that kept me company.

Bob Baxley for calling me a coward (he was right). And Christopher Konrad for calling me a MOFO (also right).

All the people who didn't answer my emails and feel bad about it right now.

The Avett brothers for reminding me to go all out—never do anything by half.

To Richard Stoakley, Bob Baxley, and Faisal Jawdat for feedback on the early outline.

The ever-brave chapter review crew: Faisal Jawdat, Robin Jeffries (Google), Bryan Zug, James Refill, and Bob Baxley.

To teachers and mentors: Todd Berkun, Rob Elkins, Jerry Reinstein, Adam Stein, Don Cole, Wilfred Seig, Joe Belfiore, Chris Jones, Steve Capps, and Mark Ashley.

The King County library system and the elves who make inter-library book loans possible.

For lending me time: Jeff Hawkins, Cory Ondrejka, Ian Phillips, Neil Enns, Stephen Rosenthal, Mark Colburn, Prasadi de Silva, Gary Flake, Derek Bates, John Musser, Richard Stoakley (Overcastmedia.com), Kenneth Norton, Kevin Schofield, Lynn Cherny, Erin McKean, Greg Linden, Adam Green, Matt Conway, Josh Strater, Brian Hutchinson, Ross Andrus, Mike Vance, Sachin Bhatia, Ian White, Paul Sauruzi, Saul Griffith, Joshua Schauer, Gaurav Oberoi & Chuck Groom (Billmonk.com), Hillel Cooperman (Jacksonfish.com), Piero Sierra, David Hounsell (CMU), John Li (menuism.com), Steve Capps, Sarah Nelson, and Josh Orum (and those names forgotten in the loss of Moleskine #7 on Continental Flight 1739; godspeed, little doodle).

For permissions, advice, blog comments and other bits of goodness: Mark Denovich, Carrie Devine, Gregory Raiz, James Bullock, Timothy Johnson, Jeff De Cagna, Powel Brodzinksi, Courtney Center, Dan Saffer, Brian Jepson, Jim Kalbach, Kevin Morrill, Rami Nasser, Eric Nehrlick, Peter Cavallo, Hanif Rehman, Catarina Flake, Dion Hinchcliffe, Jay Zipursky, Justin Martinstein, Noah Brier, Konrad West, Alexis Leon, Jason Fried, Bill Stevenson, Rory O'Connor, Gernot D Ross, John Jantos, Sam Greenfield (wiseass), Rob Lefferts, Leddom Lefferts, Shawn Murphy, Phil "5 card stud" Simon, Chris "cycling is not a sport" McGee, Mike "spin-move" Viola, David "pretty boy" Sanberg, Joe "gourmet" Mirza, and the ever-resplendent Richard "Chinaski" Grudman.

Music listened to during the writing of this book: Wonderful Smith, Neutral Milk Hotel, Avett Brothers (constantly), Arcade Fire, Johnny Cash, The Shins, Thelonious Monk, Mozart, Beethoven, Bell X1, Cat Power, Aimee Mann, The Breeders, Belly, Cake, Paul Cantelon, Elliott Smith, The Gossip, Jack Johnson, King Missile, Velvet Underground, Frank Sinatra, The Long Winters, REM, Radiohead, Social Distortion, Woody Guthrie, Bruce Springsteen, Sleater-Kinney, Regina Spektor, and Cut Chemists.

About the author

Scott Berkun worked on the Internet Explorer team at Microsoft from 1994–1999 and left the company in 2003 with the goal of writing enough books to fill this shelf. This is his second book; he wrote the 2005 bestseller *The Art of Project Management* (O'Reilly).

He makes a living writing, speaking, and teaching. He teaches a graduate course in creative thinking at the University of Washington; runs the sacred places architecture tour at NYC's GEL conference; and writes about innovation, design, and management at *www.scottberkun.com*.

Index

Colophon

The cover image is from Getty Images. The cover fonts are Ben-tonSans and Sabon. The text font is Sabon; the heading font is BentonSans.

Page numbers were hand-carved, based on a Dutch interpretation of a sketch of reproductions of a famous 13th-century Chinese monograph series believed to have been glanced at once by Marco Polo's best friend's sister. Note the glory of the sans-serifed ascenders! They cost extra, you know.

Certain complex interior layout was performed remotely from on-board the International Space Station using—according to the police report—laser beams, an unidentified space gas, and a case of Russian beer.

The ink that makes up these very words was extracted from thousands of adolescent Malaysian juniper beetles, hand-picked for their deep black hues. Blended with tonic water from the Bavarian Alps (northern, not that southern swill), this priceless ink is then stored in the finest French hardwood kegs, which are wrapped in a layer of Egyptian velvet and left to age for centuries while a secret tribe of the world's finest chorally trained children bless them with chants of salvation for all those who read words in col-ophons written in this ink.

This book, except for ink, fonts, and page numbers, is made from 99% recycled Grade A truffle compost, approved by the International Order of Colophon Authors (IOCA). The remaining 1% was, tragically, only semi-recycled truffle compost that did not meet final level-3 IOCA approval. I am as devastated as you.

I'd like to interrupt this colophon to apologize for our inability to provide the high quality of colophon you have come to expect from O'Reilly. Please believe that we did everything to prevent this from happening. Several recommended colophonists were hired, found unworthy, replaced, fired, shoved (en masse, out of spite), scantily clad, into cold, dark corners and made to read *War and Peace*, in Russian, backward, until finally, at great expense, this colophonist was rightfully chosen to free the imprisoned practitioners of colophon arts and save the day.

Before you go, know that I, anonymous colophon writer, have spared the human race from certain extinction dozens of times through use of my varied colophonic powers. Out of respect, you should always read colophons—you never know what you might find.